AN INTRODUCTION TO THE LAW OF EMPLOYMENT DISCRIMINATION

Michael Evan Gold

ILR Bulletin 68

ILR Press
New York State School of Industrial and Labor Relations
Cornell University

Library of Congress Cataloging-in-Publication Data

Gold, Michael Evan.
An introduction to the law of employment discrimination / Michael Evan Gold.
p.   cm. — (ILR bulletin ; 68)
Includes index.
ISBN 0-87546-311-8 (pbk.)

1. Discrimination in employment—Law and legislation—United States. I. Title. II.
Series: Bulletin (New York State School of Industrial and Labor Relations); no. 68.
KF3464.G55 1993
344.73'01133—dc20
[347.3041133]   93–15078

Copies of this bulletin can be ordered from
ILR Press
School of Industrial and Labor Relations
Cornell University
Ithaca, NY 14853-3901

Telephone 607/255-2264

Printed in the United States of America

5 4 3 2 1

Contents

Preface

Purpose of This Bulletin

America is called the land of opportunity, but for the first 350 years of our history we denied equality of opportunity to most of our citizens. From the landing on Plymouth Rock to the middle of the twentieth century, the best of everything was reserved for men with white skin. Then a sea change occurred, a change that makes proud everyone who contributed to it and even those who merely witnessed it. America began to fulfill its promise.

The fulfillment began in 1957 when Rosa Parks refused to move to the back of a bus one afternoon in Montgomery, Alabama. She was tired—physically tired from her job and emotionally tired from the burden of racial segregation. Her defiance of injustice marked the beginning of the civil rights movement and inspired Martin Luther King, Jr., to organize a boycott of the buses in Montgomery. King went on to organize many other non-violent protests against racial discrimination. He led the greatest moral movement in our history.

Influenced by this movement, John F. Kennedy assumed the presidency in 1961 with the goal of ensuring equality of opportunity to all Americans, regardless of race or sex. Kennedy's administration took a step toward this goal by supporting the Equal Pay Act of 1963; it became law and now prohibits employers from paying a woman less than a man when they perform equal work. The Equal Pay Act is the first in a series of federal laws that guarantee equality of opportunity in employment.

Kennedy's administration also supported perhaps the most important civil rights legislation of this century. The bill applied to voting, to public accommodations such as hotels and restaurants, to public schools, and to employment. Kennedy was assassinated while Congress was considering the bill, but his successor, Lyndon B. Johnson, made its passage his top priority. Despite the longest debate in the history of the Senate, Congress passed the Civil Rights Act in 1964. Title VII of this law prohibits employment discrimination on the grounds of race, color, religion, sex, or national origin.

During the debates in Congress on Title VII, it was suggested that the bill be expanded to prohibit age discrimination. Instead, Congress instructed the Secretary of Labor to study the issue and report in two years. The report recommended action, and in 1967 Congress passed and President Johnson signed the Age Discrimination in Employment Act. Today this law prohibits age discrimination against any worker aged forty or older.

Congress turned its attention to other employment issues after the flurry of antidiscrimination legislation of the mid-1960s. Yet our legislators have remained sensitive to the problem of discrimination. Title VII has been amended to increase the number of workers protected against race and sex discrimination and to overrule restrictive decisions of the Supreme Court. But more than tinkering was necessary because the law omitted protection for the most vulnerable of all workers and potential workers: the disabled. This omission was rectified when the Americans with Disabilities Act of 1990 became law. Today most workers with disabilities are protected against discrimination if their disabilities do not affect their job performance; in addition, employers are obligated to make reasonable changes to jobs and the work environment to accommodate workers whose disabilities do affect their job performance.

The purpose of this bulletin is to summarize the principal federal laws against employment discrimination. We hope it serves as a contribution to the effort to achieve equality of opportunity for every worker.

Scope of This Bulletin

This bulletin summarizes the federal laws that prohibit employment discrimination on the basis of race, color, religion, sex, national origin, age, and disability. Many state and local laws also prohibit employment discrimination. Those laws are valid, and in many cases they give more protection to workers than the federal laws do; however, this bulletin focuses on the federal law. Also, federal laws forbid discrimination in other areas—for example, in voting, housing, and schools; but this bulletin is limited to discrimination in employment. (For convenience, the word "discrimination" is often used alone, without the qualifying word "employment"; nevertheless, the reader should understand that this bulletin deals only with employment discrimination.)

With regard to the substantive law—that is, what is permitted or prohibited—the rules are the same for every covered employer; this bulletin summarizes those rules. With regard to the procedural law—that is, the methods for enforcing the substantive law—the procedures vary. One set of procedures must be used to enforce the law against private employers and state and local governments; this bulletin describes those procedures. Another set of procedures must be used to enforce the law against the federal government; this bulletin does not cover those procedures. Federal employees are advised to consult the equal employment officer in their agencies about the relevant procedures.

The four statutes which this bulletin summarizes—Title VII of the Civil Rights Act of 1964, the Age Discrimination in Employment Act of 1967, the Americans with Disabilities Act of 1990, and the Equal Pay Act of 1963—are long and complex. The decisions interpreting these statutes, rendered by the Equal Employment Opportunity Commission and by the courts, fill many volumes of books. As a result, only the most important areas of the law are discussed in this bulletin, and the discussion of these areas is often simplified. Although all of the following statements about the law are accurate, many are incomplete. Much more could be said about every topic discussed in this bulletin.

Who Should Read This Bulletin and Who Should Not

Two types of reader are likely to benefit from reading this bulletin. One is the person who knows little or nothing about the law. The other is the person whose knowledge has become rusty or out of date. The former can learn, and the latter can relearn, the basic principles and structure of the law.

One type of reader is unlikely to benefit from this bulletin: the person who needs to know whether specific conduct, arising in a context of many other facts, is legal or illegal. Too many rules have been omitted and too many qualifications have gone unstated for this bulletin to serve that purpose. The reader who needs to know how the law applies to a specific case should consult a comprehensive treatise on the relevant statute or, better yet, a lawyer.

A Note on Names

In this bulletin we attempt to refer to groups of people by the names they wish us to use or by the names they call themselves. For this reason, this bulletin refers to people of African descent as "African-Americans" and to people of Asian descent as "Asian-Americans."

People whose forebears lived in Latin America refer to themselves sometimes as "Hispanic-Americans" and sometimes as "Latino-Americans." We use the latter term, which has the rich flavor of the Spanish language that so many Latino-Americans speak.

People descended from the pre-Colonial inhabitants of America have long been called "Indians," and many still call themselves by this name. But, in addition to reflecting Columbus's mistaken belief that the Western Hemisphere was India, this term can be confusing when people from India are involved. The term "Native American" is often used today, and the term "Amerindian" is gaining currency. We use the former because it seems to be used more often and is parallel in construction to the other names used herein.

The term "people of color" is a handy way to include all the peoples so far named. It is especially convenient in the expression "women and people of color," which incorporates all the oppressed classes that Title VII was enacted to protect. "Minorities" may be used more often, but, if demographic trends continue, today's minorities will be soon be tomorrow's majority.

Americans of European provenance commonly call themselves "white." This term became accepted as a replacement for "Caucasian" at the time that "black" replaced "Negro." But "white" is truly descriptive only of Northern Europeans, and many Latino-Americans are as white as any Southern Europeans. For these reasons, and because it is parallel to the other names used herein, we use the term "European-Americans." We realize that the terms "white" and "people of color" are natural opposites, and we acknowledge the inconsistency of our using the former but not the latter. If that is the only error in this bulletin, we will rejoice.

A Note on Agency

An important principle applies to all the federal laws against discrimination, namely, the principle of agency. It holds the owner of a business responsible for the actions of employees, especially supervisors. Similarly, the government is responsible for the actions of its officials, and a labor union is responsible for the actions of its representatives. Therefore, an employer, a union, or an agency of the government cannot escape responsibility by arguing that an act of discrimination was unauthorized or against policy. If the individual who does an act is empowered by the employer, union, or government to do the act—for example, to discharge an employee or to deny a grievance—the employer, union, or government is responsible if the act is illegal.

1
Title VII of the Civil Rights Act of 1964

Title VII of the Civil Rights Act of 1964, as amended, is our basic law against employment discrimination. This chapter explains who is protected by Title VII and who must heed it. This chapter also identifies the kinds of actions that Title VII outlaws (that is, the varieties of illegal discrimination), the remedies for discrimination, and the procedures for bringing a claim under the statute.

Who Is Protected by Title VII

Title VII prohibits employment discrimination against employees and applicants for employment on the basis of race, color, religion, sex, or national origin. Common-sense definitions of these categories are correct in large part. Race means Caucasian, Negro, Oriental. Color means white, black, brown. Religion means Protestant, Catholic, Jewish. Sex means man, woman. (Sex includes pregnancy but does not include sexual preference. Title VII does not protect workers against discrimination based on their homosexuality.)

The meaning of national origin may be surprising. Under Title VII, national origin does not refer to a worker's citizenship; instead, it refers to the country in which a worker or one's ancestors were born. Thus, suppose Regina is not an American citizen, but she has permission to work in this country. An employer would violate Title VII by refusing to hire her because she or her ancestors were born in Mexico (her national origin), but would not violate Title VII by refusing to hire her because she is not an American citizen. (If Regina had applied for citizenship, however, this employer would be violating the Immigration Reform and Control Act of 1986. It protects United States citizens, and aliens in the process of becoming citizens, from discrimination based on citizenship.)

Every worker is protected by Title VII in several ways. Each individual has a race, a color, a religion (or lack of one), a sex, and a national origin, and so each of us is protected from discrimination based on race, color, religion, sex, and national origin. Although the law was passed primarily to protect women and people of color from discrimination, Congress intended to protect all of us. As a result, European-Americans as well as African-Americans are protected against discrimination based on race or color. Men as well as women are protected from discrimination based on sex. Protestants as well as Catholics, Jews, and Moslems are protected from discrimination based on religion.

United States citizens working abroad for United States employers or for foreign companies controlled by United States employers are also protected.

For convenience, in this chapter we will speak of discrimination because of "race or sex," which are the most frequent kinds of discrimination. The reader should understand, however, that we mean this term to include discrimination because of color, religion, and national origin as well.

Who Must Obey Title VII

Title VII covers private employers who have fifteen or more employees. Small private employers, therefore, are not covered. Title VII covers public employers—federal, state, and local governments and their agencies—regardless of the number of employees they have.

Title VII covers labor unions that have fifteen or more members or that operate a hiring hall that supplies workers to a covered employer. Title VII also covers employment agencies that refer workers to covered employers.

Title VII covers religious institutions (for example, churches, clubs, and parochial schools) but contains a specific exception allowing them to discriminate in favor of members of their religion. Thus, religious institutions may not discriminate against workers on the grounds of race, color, sex, or national origin. A Baptist church that needs a secretary may require that all applicants be Baptists, but the church may not refuse to hire a male Baptist because of his sex.

Most Title VII lawsuits have been brought against private employers. For this reason, and for convenience, most of the examples in this chapter will describe discrimination by private employers. But the reader should bear in mind that the principles discussed in this bulletin also apply to public employers, labor unions, and employment agencies.

The Idea of Discrimination

What is discrimination? In English, the root word "discriminate" carries a range of meanings. Some of them are positive, as in, "She is a woman of discriminating taste"; and some of them are negative, as in, "The police officer discriminated against African-American suspects."

All senses of the word have in common the act of distinguishing one thing from another. If the things are truly different, and the difference justifies treating them differently, the discrimination is legitimate. If the things are not different, or the difference does not justify treating them differently, the discrimination is not legitimate. Thus, suppose a parent allows a seventeen-year-old to stay out until midnight but requires a thirteen-year-old to be home by 10 o'clock. The children are different, and the difference in their ages (and, presumably, their judgment) justifies the discrimination in curfews.

Now suppose the parent allows the seventeen-year-old to choose which program to watch on television every night, regardless of what the thirteen-year-old desires. The desires of the children to choose which programs to watch are equally legitimate, so the discrimination is unjustified.

Finally, suppose the seventeen-year-old wishes to try out for the girls' basketball team, while the thirteen-year-old wishes to try out for the boys' soccer team; and, although both are good athletes, the parent enthusiastically supports the boy but disheartens the girl. There are differences between basketball and soccer, and between a boy and a girl; but these differences do not justify encouraging the one and discouraging the other, so the discrimination is unjustified.

The legal meanings of "discrimination" draw on its English meaning, but the reader should bear in mind that, like many other terms, the legal and English meanings of "discrimination" are not identical. Many people might agree that a given act is discriminatory in the English sense of the word, but the act might not be illegal; conversely, an act that is illegal might not seem to be discriminatory in its English sense. Thus, the parent who encourages a son to play sports but discourages a daughter has, in ordinary usage, discriminated against the daughter; but no law has been violated. An employer who hires men and women of all races, based solely on their scores on intelligence tests, may actually be violating the law but has not discriminated in the usual sense of the word. In this bulletin, we shall concentrate on the legal meanings of "discrimination." As we shall see, Title VII contains four definitions of discrimination.

Disparate Treatment

The first definition of discrimination has become known as "disparate treatment," which means intentionally denying an opportunity to a worker because of race or sex. If a union refuses to admit Laura to membership because it "already has enough women," it is guilty of disparate treatment of women. If an employer refuses to promote Black, a qualified African-American, to a supervisory job because of her race, the employer is guilty of disparate treatment.

If a reason other than race or sex motivates the decision, the employer is not guilty of disparate treatment. Thus, suppose Isadore and Ilene apply for a job. Ilene is better qualified, but the employer hires Isadore because he is the employer's nephew. This employer is not guilty of disparate treatment; the employer denied Ilene the job, not because of her sex, but because of Isadore's family status.

The Role of Intent

As the examples above illustrate, the key to disparate treatment is intent. It is illegal to deny an employment opportunity *because of* race or sex. In many cases, intent is easy to understand. We have no doubt about the intent of the union that refuses to admit any woman to membership or the employer who refuses to promote an African-American to supervisor.

Sometimes, however, the question of intent is more difficult. For example, suppose the employer offers this explanation for refusing to promote Black to supervisor: "I am not prejudiced, but I was afraid that my workers would not take orders from a person of color." Did this employer intend to deny Black an opportunity because of her race? The answer is yes. The employer's specific reason was Black's race; the reason underlying the employer's reason is irrelevant.

Another difficult case of intent involves mixed or multiple motives. Suppose the employer says, "I did not promote Black because she was frequently absent from work *and* because she is an African-American." The first of these reasons is legal; the second is not. Did this employer intentionally discriminate against Black because of her race? Once again, the answer is yes. If any one of an employer's reasons is illegal, the employer has broken the law.

Examples of Disparate Treatment

Pension Benefits Insurance companies keep separate statistics on men and women; as a result, we know that men are greater risks for some purposes and women are for others. Consider the effect of longevity, for example. Women on average outlive men of the same age. To a *life insurance* program, the man is a greater risk than the woman because he is likely to die sooner. But to a *pension* program, the woman is the greater risk because she will probably outlive the man and, consequently, draw benefits for a longer period of time.

The traditional way for insurance programs to deal with differential risks has been to charge a higher premium to the group with the higher risk. For example, young drivers have more automobile accidents than middle-aged drivers, and insurance companies charge the young drivers higher premiums.

It was natural for pension plans to use the same approach to deal with longevity. On average, a woman at retirement age will outlive a man by five years. Thus, if monthly pension benefits are equal for male and female counterparts (persons of the same age and with the same employment histories), she will collect more total money than he will. Managers of pension plans thought it was unfair that the woman should receive greater benefits when she and the man had served the company for the same length of time and made identical contributions to the plan. Accordingly, the managers required women to contribute more to their pension plans; the extra money that the average woman received in retirement was balanced by the extra money she contributed as a worker.

A woman named Manhart sued, arguing that it was disparate treatment to charge a woman a higher premium for a pension than her male counterpart was charged. The Supreme Court agreed with her. Averages, said the Court, are true for groups; the pension plan's argument was correct only if one looked at groups of men and women. But Title VII requires equal treatment for individuals. Looking at individuals, we find that some women outlive their male counterparts, but some do not; and it is unfair to treat all women as though they will outlive their counterparts. Individual justice requires that each woman pay the same monthly contribution as her male counterpart pays.

In the past, some pension plans dealt with women's longer life expectancy in another way: they collected equal contributions from male and female counterparts but paid the woman lower monthly (yet equal lifetime) benefits. When a woman named Norris challenged this practice, the Supreme Court struck it down.

Pregnancy   Another case involved medical insurance benefits for women during pregnancy. An employer provided comprehensive medical insurance coverage, excluding only pregnancy. When Ms. Gilbert sued her employer, she argued that the plan was guilty of disparate treatment because it divided men and women into separate classes and treated the women less favorably: whereas every medical expense a *man* might incur was covered, a significant expense a *woman* might incur—pregnancy—was not covered. The Supreme Court rejected this argument and upheld the plan for two reasons. First, the Court argued, the plan did not divide workers into classes of men and women; rather, the plan divided workers into classes of pregnant and nonpregnant persons. Because many women were in the class of nonpregnant persons, the plan did not treat women less favorably. Second, even if the plan did divide men and women into separate classes, pregnancy is not a disease; therefore, the medical insurance program covered diseases of men and women equally.

This reasoning was strongly criticized from many quarters. Because only women can become pregnant, it was common sense that the plan treated women less favorably than men. Motivated by common sense rather than judicial hair splitting, Congress amended Title VII specifically to overrule the Supreme Court. Today, the law does not require an employer to provide medical insurance for workers; but if medical insurance is provided, the law requires that pregnancy be treated the same as other conditions.

Does this amendment apply to the wives of male employees? In a case brought against the Newport News Shipping Company, the Supreme Court said yes. Once again, the law does not require an employer to provide medical insurance for the dependents of workers; but if insurance for dependents is provided, the pregnancy of a worker's wife must be covered to the same extent as other conditions of workers' dependents.

Discrimination because of pregnancy can occur in other ways. An employer who discharges a woman because she has a lawful abortion is guilty of discrimination. Similarly, an employer who discharges an unmarried woman because she becomes pregnant is guilty of discrimination unless the employer also discharges unwed fathers.

Sexual Harassment   Does Title VII prohibit sexual harassment? It can be argued that Title VII prohibits sex discrimination, not sexual discrimination. If an employer harasses women but not men, the argument goes, that is illegal sex discrimination; but if an employer harasses only one woman, the reason is her unique sexuality, not her sex. The counterargument is that sexual harassment has more to do with the power of men over women than with sexual attraction. Also, the woman's sex was surely part of the employer's motivation in harassing her; if she were a man, the harassment would not have occurred. In a case brought by a woman named Vinson, the Supreme Court accepted the latter argument, but not completely. Some, but not all, forms of sexual harassment violate Title VII; and the employer is liable for harassment in some, but not all, cases.

The Court drew three distinctions. The first concerns the conduct itself. Judges are reluctant to get deeply involved in relations between men and women. For this reason, only serious harassment is outlawed; occasional embarassment is not. The extremes are easily illustrated: it is illegal for an employer to demand that a woman have sex with him as a condition of keeping her job, but it is not illegal for an employer to ask a woman for a date. Of course, the area between these extremes is vast, and there is much debate about where the line should be drawn between permissible and impermissible relations. A good general guideline is that any unwelcomed sexual attention should be prohibited.

The second distinction concerns what happens to the woman when she resists, and the third concerns whether the woman complains to higher authority about the harassment. These two distinctions are related to one another. A woman who resists harassment might be deprived of an employment opportunity; for example, the employer might deny her a promotion or transfer or even fire her. This sort of case is called "quid pro quo" (in exchange for) harassment. If an agent of the employer demands that a woman provide sex as the quid pro quo for an employment opportunity, the employer is always liable, even if the agent is a low-level supervisor and even if she does not complain to higher management.

Other forms of sexual harassment are also illegal. Unwelcomed caresses, obscene comments, and the like can make a woman's working conditions unbearable, even if she is never denied a promotion or laid off. This sort of case is called "hostile environment" harassment. It is illegal, but whether the employer is liable to the woman depends on whether the company has a policy against sexual harassment and whether the woman seeks help from higher management. The idea is that the employer cannot be expected to know that a man is creating a hostile environment for a woman unless she complains about it. Therefore, if the employer establishes a policy against harassment, the woman follows the policy (for example, notifies the personnel director), and the harassment continues, the employer is responsible for it; if she does not follow the policy, she is unlikely to win in court. If the employer lacks a policy against harassment, the woman is more likely to win even if she does not seek help within the company.

Dress and Grooming Codes Many employers have different dress and grooming codes for men and women. For example, some employers permit women to wear long hair but require men to keep their hair above the collar; and some employers prohibit women from wearing pants but require men to wear them. The courts have upheld such rules, although the rationale for these decisions is not entirely clear. Perhaps the rules are not examples of disparate treatment at all, in that they require that both men and women conform to social expectations. Or perhaps the rules do not have any important effect on the terms and conditions of employment.

Some disparate rules do affect the terms of employment, however, and they are illegal. For example, it was discriminatory for an employer to require a woman to wear a revealing costume that invited sexual harassment. Similarly, it was discriminatory for an employer to require women to wear identical uniforms but to permit men to wear the business attire of their choice. These rules tended to place the women in an inferior position.

Although an employer may require women to *dress* in a basically feminine way, an employer may not require women to *act* in a feminine way. For example, Ms. Hopkins was a competent accountant and brought in business to her firm, yet it denied her a partnership because she was "too macho": she used foul language, did not wear makeup or style her hair, and generally refused to conform to stereotypes of feminine behavior. Because the firm judged her according to stereotypes, not performance, the Supreme Court found it guilty of sex discrimination.

Spouses Suppose an employer offers to hire a European-American man but, upon learning that he is married to an African-American woman, decides to withdraw the offer. Has the employer violated Title VII? It could be argued that the cause of the employer's decision was not the man's race but the woman's; and because she is not an employee or an applicant, she is not protected by Title VII. This argument is fallacious, however, because the man's race was part of the employer's motivation. If the man had been a different race (in this example, an African-American), he would have been hired; *he* is protected by the law, and, therefore, he was discriminated against because of his race.

Proving Intent Traditional Ways

Because disparate treatment occurs only when an employer or a union acts from an illegal motive, the judge in each disparate treatment case must decide why the defendant denied the opportunity to the plaintiff. Intent can be established in a disparate treatment case in one of three ways. Two of them are traditional, and the third uses statistics.

Direct Evidence Occasionally, a plaintiff can give a judge a glimpse into a defendant's state of mind. Hollywood-style confessions on the witness stand are uncommon, but a defendant might have made damaging admissions outside of court in front of someone who is willing to testify. In one case, several women were responsible for normal cleaning in a plant. Most of the women were African-Americans, but one was a European-American. One day their supervisor assigned the African-Americans to heavy cleaning that was outside their job description. He told the European-American to continue with her normal duties. When the African-Americans protested, the supervisor said, "Colored people should stay in their places." He also said, "Colored folks are hired to clean because they clean better." Such statements have been traditionally accepted as direct evidence of the defendant's intent.

Comparative Evidence In the usual case, the plaintiff has no direct evidence of the defendant's motive, and another traditional form of evidence—inference—must be used. An inference of discrimination can be established by comparing how the employer treats similarly situated workers. In a case that reached the Supreme Court, a European-American named McDonald and two African-Americans were caught stealing by their employer. No evidence suggested that McDonald was more guilty than the African-Americans (for example, he was not the ringleader); therefore, all three employees were similarly situated. Nevertheless, McDonald was discharged while the African-Americans were retained. By comparing his treatment with that of the African-Americans, McDonald proved that the employer discriminated against him.

***McDonnell Douglas* Formula** In many cases, a plaintiff cannot identify a specific person with whom to compare oneself. Nevertheless, an inference of discrimination may be possible. For cases involving discrimination against a single person, the Supreme Court approved the following formula in the *McDonnell Douglas* case: if the plaintiff proves that

(1) the plaintiff is a woman or person of color,

(2) the plaintiff applied for a position,

(3) the position was vacant,

(4) the plaintiff was qualified for the position,

(5) the employer rejected the plaintiff, and

(6) the employer continued to accept applications,

an inference of illegal intent arises. The reason for the inference is that the plaintiff has ruled out the three most common legitimate reasons that a person does not get a particular position. These reasons are that the person did not apply, the person was not qualified, and the position was not open. Once these reasons are eliminated, the next most likely reason that a woman or person of color is denied an opportunity is race or sex.

To illustrate the *McDonnell Douglas* formula, suppose Wong and Alexander apply to a contractor for a job as a plumber. Alexander is hired, and Wong sues. Wong can establish an inference of intentional discrimination by proving (1) he is an Asian-American, (2) he applied for the job, (3) the job was vacant, (4) he had completed a vocational educational program in plumbing, (5) he was rejected, and (6) the contractor hired someone else.

The *McDonnell Douglas* formula was developed in a hiring case, as the examples above indicate; but the formula can be applied to other situations. It can be applied to a promotion case almost without change and is easily adapted to layoff, discharge, and discipline cases as well. Thus, suppose Wong is hired but later is laid off because he is an Asian-American. An inference of intent to discriminate will arise if he can prove that a European-American with equal or lesser qualifications or record of performance was retained in a similar job.

Rebutting Traditional Proof of Intent   So far we have examined the traditional kinds of evidence that a plaintiff can use to prove intentional discrimination. Now let us turn to the employer's evidence in traditional cases.

An employer may use two strategies. One is to show that the plaintiff's evidence is false. For example, the supervisor who said that blacks are better at cleaning than whites might have testified that he was misquoted or that his comment was taken out of context. Likewise, the contractor might testify that Wong did not submit an application for the job or did not complete the vocational educational program.

The other traditional strategy an employer may use is to present evidence of a legitimate, nondiscriminatory reason for what happened. Such a reason in the cleaners' case might have been that the European-American woman was recovering from an injury and could not perform the heavier work. In the plumber's case, the contractor might testify that she hired Alexander instead of Wong because Alexander had more experience and, therefore, was better qualified.

At the end of a trial, the judge must decide whether the plaintiff's or the defendant's evidence is more convincing. If the evidence is evenly balanced, the judge must rule for the defendant; in legal terminology, the burden of proving illegal intent is on the plaintiff.

Proving Intent with Statistics

The *McDonnell Douglas* formula is useful in a case brought by one plaintiff, but it is not helpful in a class-action case brought on behalf of a large group or class of plaintiffs. Suppose, for example, a large employer is accused of discrimination in hiring Latino-Americans. The *McDonnell Douglas* formula might establish that the employer discriminated against one or two or three individuals, but not that the employer discriminated against Latino-Americans in general. To prove that an employer intended to discriminate against a class, statistics are necessary.

Statistical Reasoning in General Statistical evidence is a complex topic, and we can only introduce the reader to it here. The heart of it is the belief that, if a given event is very unlikely to happen by chance, and it happens anyway, it was probably caused on purpose. For example, suppose Groucho and Harpo are playing poker for money. Groucho shuffles the deck, deals, and wins the first hand with four aces. He shuffles again, deals, and wins the second hand, also with four aces. He shuffles, deals, and once again wins with four aces. Harpo might have the following thoughts: "A player might get four aces in three consecutive hands, even in an honest game. This event happens by chance so rarely, however, that it probably had a specific cause. Given that Groucho was dealing and winning money on each hand, it is likely that he was cheating. So I will never speak again."

Statistical Reasoning in Disparate Treatment Cases Similar reasoning can be applied to proving intent in disparate treatment cases. If an employer hires or promotes substantially fewer women or people of color, or lays off substantially more of them, than is likely to occur by chance in a fair process, an inference arises that the employer intended to discriminate against them. A good example occurred when the government sued the Teamsters Union and a nationwide trucking company on behalf of a class of African-Americans and Latino-Americans. (The government does not bring many such suits, but any member of the class can sue on behalf of the whole class.) The company had two kinds of jobs for drivers: city driving and line driving. The jobs were basically the same except that the line drivers went on overnight trips between cities. The line jobs paid better than the city jobs. The government proved that, whereas people of color held 9 percent of the city driving jobs, they held less than 1 percent of the line driving jobs; and no persons of color were employed in some areas where people of color were as much as one-third of the population. These statistics created an inference that the employer deliberately excluded people of color from line driving jobs. Just as it was unlikely that, in a fair game, Groucho would deal himself three consecutive hands of four aces, it was unlikely that a fair employer would give all the line driving jobs to European-Americans.

An important question is the meaning of "unlikely." How do we know when it is unlikely that the percentage of women or people of color in a job is the result of fair hiring? In other words, what are the odds? The Supreme Court's answer is approximately one in one hundred. That is, if a result could occur by chance in a fair process less than one time in one hundred, an inference arises that discrimination is at work. In the drivers' case, the odds were much less than one in one hundred that, under fair hiring, persons of color would constitute 9 percent of the city drivers and less than 1 percent of the line drivers, and the odds were even lower that fair hiring would lead to no persons of color as line drivers in areas where one-third of the population was African-Americans and Latino-Americans.

The statistics in the drivers' case were straightforward. Often, however, sophisticated techniques are necessary to analyze an employer's practices. Those techniques are beyond the scope of this bulletin; but the reader should be aware that statistics can be misleading, and they must be interpreted by experts.

Rebutting Statistical Proof of Intent Showing that discrimination based on sex or race is a likely explanation of the employer's hiring practices is not the same as proving conclusively that the employer intended to discriminate against women or people of color. Statistical proof is rarely conclusive. But like the *McDonnell Douglas* formula, statistical reasoning gives rise to an inference of illegal intent.

Of course, the employer has the right to attack the plaintiffs' proof and to rebut the inference of illegal intent. Two strategies are commonly used. First, the employer may criticize the plaintiffs' statistics. Perhaps the numbers are inaccurate, or perhaps the plaintiffs' mathematical analysis is erroneous. Second, the employer may offer a legitimate reason to explain why so few members of the plaintiffs' class were hired or promoted. The employer in the drivers' case used the second strategy. Trying to explain the very small number of persons of color in line driving jobs, the employer conceded that it had discriminated in the past but said that the discrimination occurred before Title VII took effect in 1965; the employer claimed to have hired fairly after this date. The reason so few people of color held line driving jobs, argued the employer, was that the work force had been shrinking. If this explanation had been true, the employer would have won the case.

Proof of Pretext After the employer has the opportunity to prove that the plaintiffs' evidence is false, the plaintiffs have a chance to return the favor, that is, to show that the employer's evidence is pretextual or untrue. If the employer has criticized the plaintiffs' statistics, the plaintiffs may criticize the criticism. (Some Title VII cases turn into a war among expert witnesses.) If the employer has offered an explanation of why so few plaintiffs were hired or promoted, the plaintiffs may attempt to prove that the explanation is false. Thus, in the drivers' case, after the employer offered the explanation that the work force was shrinking, the government had the opportunity to demonstrate that the explanation was pretextual. The government proved that, although the total number of drivers had indeed declined, the employer had actually hired hundreds of new drivers because of turnover and that almost all the line drivers hired after Title VII took effect were European-Americans. Accordingly, the Supreme Court decided that the employer's explanation was a pretext and that the employer had intentionally discriminated against people of color in hiring for line driving jobs, and the government won the case.

Ultimately, the burden of proof on the issue of intent rests on the plaintiffs. The judge will rule for the party whose evidence is more convincing. If the evidence is evenly balanced, the judge must rule for the defendant.

Bona Fide Occupational Qualifications

Congress believed that disparate treatment can be justified in certain instances. If religion, sex, or national origin is a bona fide occupational qualification ("bfoq")—that is, a characteristic that is genuinely necessary to the performance of a job—an employer may refuse to hire anyone who lacks the necessary characteristic. For example, being a woman is a bfoq for the job of actress for the part of Cleopatra; our desire for authenticity in dramatic productions is more important than providing opportunities for men to portray women. Similarly, being Catholic can be a bfoq for a job teaching religion courses in a school that maintains a strong Catholic identity.

In a controversial case brought by a woman named Rawlinson, the Supreme Court held that the state of Alabama could lawfully prohibit women from serving as guards in state prisons for men. One way of interpreting this case (another way is suggested below) is that the Court found that women could not perform the job. The essence of the job was maintaining security. The conditions in the Alabama prisons were so bad (indeed, in another case they were held to violate the U.S. Constitution) that a female guard might be raped. Because a rape would disrupt prison security, and because any woman might be raped, the Court held that being a man was a bfoq for this job. (Women can guard male inmates in other prisons where conditions are better.)

The bfoq is an exception to the rule against discrimination based on sex, religion, or national origin. Like any other exception, it has to be kept under control so it does not swallow the rule. Thus, the courts have refused to allow customer preference to qualify as a bfoq; otherwise, an employer could easily claim that customers prefer female flight attendants or will not buy encyclopedias from Asian-American sales representatives. Such claims are rejected because allowing them would defeat the goals of breaking down unnecessary barriers and eradicating stereotypes. Likewise, a bfoq may not be based on the belief that a job is physically too difficult for a woman to perform; to the extent possible, decisions must be based on individual qualifications. Nor can a bfoq be justified on the basis that the job is too dangerous for a woman; like a man, she is entitled to decide for herself which risks to take.

A woman may be entitled to decide whether to take a risk that endangers herself, but should she also be entitled to create a risk that endangers other people? The answer depends on who the other people are. If the other people are customers or co-workers, and if a woman's very sex poses a risk to them, an employer may exclude her from the job. Another way of interpreting the guard's case is that the Supreme Court permitted Alabama to prohibit women from guarding men in state prisons because an attack on a woman guard would endanger other guards as well as inmates.

If the person endangered is the embryo or fetus that a female worker is or might be carrying, the opposite result has been reached. In a case against the Johnson Controls Company, the Supreme Court held that being male is not a bfoq for a job that might endanger a woman's offspring. The Court invalidated the employer's policy of prohibiting fertile women from working around lead, even though it can cause birth defects.

Two further comments about bfoq's are in order. First, Title VII does not allow race or color to qualify as a bfoq. Second, the burden of proof is on the employer to establish that religion, sex, or national origin is a bfoq for a particular job.

Affirmative Action and Reverse Discrimination

"Affirmative action" refers to actions that are aimed at increasing the numbers of women and people of color in a work force. These actions range from the soft to the hard, from advertising jobs in Spanish to filling a rigid quota. Of whatever variety, affirmative action is a kind of disparate treatment, for the employer takes certain action because of applicants' race or sex.

Affirmative action is never *required* by Title VII (except in unusual cases as part of a remedy ordered by a court for proven discrimination). Some kinds of affirmative action are *permitted* by law, however, and some are not.

The purpose of Title VII conflicts in a way with the specific words of the statute. The purpose is to enhance employment opportunities for women and people of color; affirmative action is consistent with this purpose. But the words of the statute prohibit discrimination against anyone because of race or sex; affirmative action violates the literal meaning of these words. In harmonizing the purpose and the words of the law, the Supreme Court has held that affirmative action is lawful so long as

(1) it is based on a plan,

(2) it is intended to correct a conspicuous imbalance of women or people of color in certain jobs due to discrimination in the past,

(3) it provides reasonable protection for the interests of the other sex and races, and

(4) it will end when its goal is achieved.

All the criteria were satisfied, and the Court approved the affirmative action plan, in a case arising in Louisiana. An employer and a union at a manufacturing plant agreed to admit equal numbers of African-American and European-American workers into a skills training program. Admission was based on seniority within racial groups. It was possible, therefore, that African-Americans who stood at the top of their list might be accepted for training before European-Americans who had worked for the company for longer time but stood low on their list. Applying the four criteria, (1) the Court found that the employer and the union were following a specific plan. They were not awarding opportunities every now and then as the spirit moved them, nor were they acting on a generalized idea of doing good. (2) Less than 2 percent of the skilled trade workers in the plant were African-Americans, while they constituted nearly 40 percent of the population of the area around the plant. They had been discriminatorily excluded from the skilled trades in this area for generations. Accordingly, the plan was plainly intended to correct an imbalance that resulted from discrimination in the past, thereby satisfying the second criterion. (3) Half the positions in the training program were awarded to European-Americans, and no European-American was ousted from a job to make room for an African-American. Thus, the interests of the other race were adequately protected. (4) The plan was scheduled to terminate when the percentage of African-Americans holding skilled jobs in the plant equaled the percentage of African-Americans in the population. The plan was intended to achieve, not to preserve, a balanced work force. All four criteria having been met, Weber, the European-American who sued because an African-American with less seniority preceded him into the training program, lost his case.

The Supreme Court has also approved a somewhat different affirmative action plan. A woman was promoted to the skilled craft job of dispatcher; she was fully qualified for the position, but she ranked slightly lower than a man named Johnson on performance evaluations. It was evident that the employer had promoted the woman in part because of her sex, and Johnson sued. Again applying the four criteria, (1) the Court found the employer had a written plan that identified imbalances of women and people of color in certain groups of jobs and that contained specific goals. (2) Women were more than 36 percent of the labor pool in the area; however, they had traditionally been excluded from skilled craft jobs in the past, and they held none of the employer's craft jobs. The plan was created to redress these imbalances. (3) The interests of men were not unduly affected. The job of dispatcher was not reserved for women; rather, sex was an additional factor that the employer took into account. Also, the man who was passed over did not have a firm expectation that he would get the promotion, and he did not lose his job, his seniority, or his pay. (4) The plan lacked a termination date. This lack might well have doomed the plan, but it passed muster because no jobs were reserved for women; men were eligible for all opportunities. The Court was willing to assume that once the goal of the plan was achieved, the employer would no longer take sex into consideration. The Court probably would not make the same assumption regarding a plan in which the dominant race or sex was absolutely excluded from certain opportunities.

Preference for a woman or person of color based on goodwill but not on a carefully designed plan is illegal under Title VII. Thus, an employer who hires an African-American instead of a better qualified European-American "because we don't have enough African-Americans around here" or "because our work force is not racially balanced and we might get sued" violates the law. Also, Title VII specifically prohibits an employer from altering the results of selection tests to ensure that sufficient numbers of women or people of color pass the test.

Disparate Impact

The second legal meaning of discrimination is known as "disparate impact." (Unfortunately, "disparate impact" sounds very much like "disparate treatment," and the reader will have to concentrate to avoid confusing these different definitions of discrimination.) Whereas disparate *treatment* focuses on the *reasons* for an employer's behavior, disparate *impact* is concerned primarily with the *effects* of behavior. The basic idea of disparate impact is that an employment practice should affect various classes of people in the same way; if a practice has a proportionally greater adverse effect on one class than on another, a good reason should justify this effect.

To take a simple example, suppose equal numbers of men and women apply for a job. The employer gives all applicants a written test and hires those with the highest scores. If approximately equal numbers of each sex are hired, the employment practice (hiring by test scores) affects the classes of men and women similarly, and there is no cause for concern. But suppose twice as many men as women are hired. Something seems amiss. The test has a disparate impact on women, and it seems reasonable to require the employer to prove that the test is necessary to the business. If the test truly measures ability to perform the job, using the test is important to the business. It is unfortunate that women are not as qualified for the job as men; nonetheless, an employer is entitled to hire the best qualified workers. But if the test does not measure job-related ability (for example, suppose the test assumes the applicant is familiar with the rules of football), using the test is not necessary to the business, and it would be unfair for the employer to exclude women because of their low scores.

Proving Disparate Impact

What is a disparate impact? Although the courts have not given the final answer, a widely used standard is the "⅘" or "80 percent" rule. According to this rule, a disparate impact occurs if the success rate of the plaintiffs' class is less than ⅘ or 80 percent of the success rate of the favored class.

A hypothetical case illustrates this standard in operation. Suppose that, over a year, 1,000 Native Americans and 2,000 European-Americans apply for 1,000 vacancies in the job of clerk in a chain of grocery stores in a city. The employer gives each applicant a written aptitude test and hires those who score seventy points or higher; 800 European-Americans and 200 Native Americans are hired.

Does the aptitude test have a disparate impact on Native Americans? Because 800 of 2,000 European-Americans passed the test, their success rate is (800 ÷ 2,000 =) 40 percent; because 200 of 1,000 Native Americans passed the test, their success rate is (200 ÷ 1,000 =) 20 percent. Now these success rates must be compared. Is the Native Americans' rate at least ⅘ or 80 percent of the European-Americans' rate? We answer this question by dividing the Native Americans' success rate by the European-Americans' success rate: 20 (Native Americans' rate) ÷ 40 (European-Americans' rate) = ½ or 50 percent. This is less than the standard of ⅘ or 80 percent; consequently, the aptitude test has a disparate impact on Native Americans.

Employment practices as well as scored tests can have disparate impacts. For example, in the prison guard's case, the employer required that all guards stand at least five feet, two inches tall. (This requirement was not related to the bfoq issue discussed above.) The height requirement had a disparate impact on women, who tend to be shorter than men.

Another common employment practice that can have a disparate impact is an education requirement, for instance, a high school diploma. In a case filed by a man named Griggs, the Supreme Court held that an employer's education requirement had a disparate impact on African-Americans.

The burden is on the plaintiffs to prove that an employment practice has a disparate impact on their class. If they do not carry this burden, that is, if their evidence does not convince the judge, they will lose the case.

The early cases of disparate impact, such as the minimum height and high school diploma requirements, were straightforward. The basic idea was developed in these simple cases. Today, however, employers are aware of the idea of disparate impact: they have modified their practices, and simple cases are less likely to arise. Consider a recent case brought against the Wards Cove Packing Company. The company provided two kinds of job, seasonal and permanent. Most of the seasonal workers were people of color; most of the permanent workers were European-Americans. Does it not seem that a disparate impact occurred because people of color were concentrated in the less desirable jobs? Yet the Supreme Court held that a racially unbalanced work force, standing alone, does not prove disparate impact. The law has become complex, and one who suspects that a disparate impact exists should consult an expert.

Business Necessity

When plaintiffs complete their evidence that a practice has disparate impact on their class, the employer may attack that evidence—for example, by criticizing the plaintiffs' statistical analysis. In addition, the employer may offer a defense: the employer may seek to prove that the practice is job-related and consistent with business necessity. An employer who carries the burden of proving this defense will win the case. Even if a practice excludes a disproportional number of people in a class, the practice is legal if it serves the needs of the business.

For example, suppose a hotel is hiring bellhops and requires that applicants have never been convicted of a crime of violence or dishonesty. A class of plaintiffs proves that their class is convicted of such crimes more often than another class; as a result, the requirement excludes a disproportional number of their class. The hotel defends on the ground that bellhops have access to room keys. The hotel will win the case. Maintaining security is necessary in a hotel, and the requirement contributes to this goal because a person who has been convicted of a crime of violence or dishonesty is more likely than a law-abiding person to assault or rob a guest.

Another example is a requirement that employees be able to speak

English. Such a requirement has a disparate impact on persons born out-side the United States (for example, recent immigrants from Latin America), but it is justified by the necessity that workers communicate with the employer, other workers, and customers. (A requirement that workers be able to communicate in English must be distinguished from a requirement that workers speak English without an accent. So long as workers can make themselves understood, the requirement of accent-free English is discrimination based on national origin.)

The courts have held that paying wages in line with rates in the la-bor market is a business necessity. Women have claimed that the labor market discriminates against them and, therefore, their jobs are under-paid. For example, the going rate for a mechanic, which is a "man's job," is usually higher than the going rate for a secretary, which is a "woman's job." If these two jobs are equally valuable to a firm, and yet secretaries are paid less than mechanics, advocates of the doctrine of comparable worth believe that discrimination is occurring. They argue that the labor market is discriminating against women, and, by paying market rates, the employer is importing the discrimination into the firm. In response, employers have argued that a business cannot afford to pay women above-market rates. The federal courts have accepted the employers' ar-gument. Title VII does not recognize comparable worth. (Some state courts have been more sympathetic to women's claims, however.)

Validating a Test In the preceding examples, common sense showed us the connection between the practices under attack and the needs of the business. In many cases, however, common sense is not as helpful. Consider written tests that employers often give to applicants. The tests are supposed to identify qualified persons. Hiring qualified per-sons is certainly a need of a business, but common sense usually does not tell us whether a particular aptitude test actually identifies qualified workers. After all, some tests turn out to be worthless. Therefore, an em-ployer who uses a test that disproportionally excludes a class of people must present scientific evidence that the test really does identify quali-fied persons—in other words, that the test is valid.

Although we cannot discuss the subject in detail, we can note that a test can be validated in one of three ways. First, the employer can prove that the test predicts success on the job. This sort of proof requires the employer to develop a method of evaluating the job performance of workers. Then the employer can compare scores on the test to scores on the performance evaluation. If people who get high scores on the test also tend to get satisfactory scores on the performance evaluation, and people who get low scores on the test tend to get unsatisfactory scores on the performance evaluation, the test is valid. This method of validating a test is known as "criterion-related validation."

Another way to validate a test is called "content-related validation." It is useful when an employer can ask an applicant to perform some of the essential tasks of the job. For example, an applicant for secretary may be given a typing test, and an applicant for welder may be asked to demonstrate different kinds of welds. A secretary who cannot type or a welder who cannot weld is obviously unfit for the job.

The third way to validate a test is "construct validation." Certain qualities of personality are often thought to be necessary for a job. For example, a sales representative is supposed to be aggressive, and a social worker is supposed to be objective. A test that accurately measures qualities that are genuinely needed for a job is valid. This method of validation is rarely used, however. Tests that accurately measure qualities of personality are difficult to devise. Also, proving that a certain quality is genuinely needed for a job is difficult, for there is more than one way to skin a cat. A sales representative who is not aggressive might succeed by being sensitive to the desires of customers. Therefore, although many employers hire based on their impressions of applicants' personalities, these employers are taking a risk.

Whichever form of validation is used, the test must be validated for the job in question. Proof that a test is valid for another job, even if the titles of the jobs are similar, usually does not prove that the test is valid for the plaintiffs' job. An interesting issue concerns proof that a test is valid, not for the plaintiffs' job, but for a job higher up the ladder of progression. Suppose an employer can prove that a test validly predicts success on job 2, but the test is used for hiring into job 1. If workers automatically move up the ladder from job 1 to job 2, and if promotions occur in a relatively short period of time, the proof is acceptable. If promotion is not automatic, however, or if many workers remain in job 1 for a significant length of time, the proof is not acceptable.

Seniority

Title VII specifically provides that an employer may abide by a bona fide seniority system. A seniority system uses length of service to award employment opportunities such as raises in pay, promotions, and protection from layoffs. "Bona fide" means good faith; for present purposes, it means "without an intent to discriminate." A seniority system that is adopted and applied without an intent to discriminate is legal.

This provision is important because a seniority system can have a disparate impact on women or people of color. If they have been recently hired for a job, they will have low seniority; and if a layoff becomes necessary, the typical seniority system (last hired, first fired) puts proportionally more of them out of work. An employer or union that follows seniority in such a situation would be guilty of disparate impact discrimination if Title VII did not explicitly protect bona fide seniority systems.

A seniority system that is not bona fide is not protected by the statute. If a system is adopted or applied with the intent to put women or people of color at a disadvantage, it is illegal.

In the past, intent to discriminate was often apparent on the face of the system, for example, one that credited European-Americans' years of service but did not credit African-Americans' service. Today, evidence of intent to discriminate is more likely to lurk in the background. Thus, suppose job M used to be open to men only; job B used to be open to both sexes, but in practice it was staffed almost exclusively by women. For many years, the seniority system provided that, in the event of layoffs, a worker in job M had bumping rights to (that is, could displace workers from) job B. A few years after Title VII takes effect, job M is opened to both sexes; women are hired into job M, and men begin going into job B. Then a recession begins, and orders for the company's products start to decline. At this time, the seniority system is amended so that workers in job M can bump into job B only if they have at least five years of service in job M. On its face, the amendment does not discriminate against women; it does not say that only men can bump. But because women were denied access to job M in the past, no woman will have bumping rights for several years; thus, the effect of the amendment is to prohibit women now in job M from bumping workers (many of whom are now men) out of job B. The background of the amendment reveals that its true purpose was exactly this effect, namely, to protect men from being bumped by women. For this reason, the amendment is not bona fide.

Reasonable Accommodation to Religion

Title VII treats religion differently from race, sex, and national origin in one important way. An employer must not only refrain from discrimination based on religion but must also make reasonable accommodation to religious observances. Reasonable accommodation need not, however, subject the employer to undue hardship. Let us look more closely at this third definition of discrimination.

Definition of Religion

The term "religion" includes organized faiths such as Christianity, Judaism, and Islam, as well as subdivisions of these faiths, such as Catholicism, Episcopalianism, and Eastern Orthodoxism. "Religion" also includes individual faiths, as well as atheism and agnosticism. Thus, an employer may not require a person to engage in daily prayer or to attend religious services if the person objects. But religion does not include social or political organizations such as the Ku Klux Klan, the Masons, or the Republican party.

Duty to Make Reasonable Accommodation

If a worker informs an employer of a conflict between the worker's religion and a duty of the job, the employer must make a reasonable accommodation to the worker's religion. Reasonableness depends on the specific facts of each case, so that what is reasonable in one situation might be unreasonable in another. Nevertheless, some general rules have emerged. One is that an employer may not refuse to hire an applicant on the ground that the applicant's religious practices would require the employer to make reasonable accommodation. Title VII requires the employer to hire without regard to religion (except in the rare case in which religion is a bfoq, which is discussed below) and to make reasonable accommodation to workers' religions; an employer may not escape these duties by refusing to hire someone whose religion would require a reasonable accommodation.

Another general rule is that an employer need not accept a *worker's* proposed accommodation merely because it is reasonable; instead, the issue is whether the *employer's* proposal is reasonable. Thus, pursuant to a collective bargaining agreement, a school district allowed teachers to be absent three days each year with pay to observe religious holidays. Additional paid absences were permitted for other purposes, but these days could not be taken on religious holidays. The religion of a teacher named Philbrook required him to miss six days a year; he used his three paid religious days and proposed that the district allow him to use some of his other paid days. The district refused but allowed him to take unpaid absences. He sued on the ground that the district had refused to accept his proposal. The Supreme Court held that, because the school's accommodation was reasonable, the case was closed. The school had no duty to show that it could not adopt the teacher's proposal.

Undue Hardship

An employer need not bear undue hardship in order to accommodate a worker's religion. Like reasonable accommodation, undue hardship depends on the specific facts of each case, but some general statements can be made. In a case brought by a man named Hardison, the
Supreme Court held that an employer need not spend any money to accommodate to a worker's religious practices. For example, if a worker
wants to observe an annual religious holiday that falls on one of the
worker's regularly scheduled workdays, the employer must allow—and
perhaps help—the worker arrange an exchange of shifts with a willing
co-worker; but the employer need not offer premium pay to a co-worker
(even if the religious worker would pay the premium), assign a co-worker
to do the work, or accept an exchange with a co-worker who is unquali-
fied for the job.

Workers who request leave on a few religious holidays are less of a
problem for employers than workers who regularly observe the Sabbath
on Friday or Saturday. These latter workers, known as Sabbatarians, are
not automatically entitled to be absent on their Sabbath. If the
Sabbatarian's work can as easily be performed on another day, the employer will normally be expected to accommodate; the same is true if
other workers, in order to have Sunday off, are willing to work on Friday
or Saturday, or if the Sabbatarian can be transferred to a department in
which work on Friday or Saturday is not required. But if the
Sabbatarian's job requires work on the Sabbath, the employer need not
do without that work or pay extra for another worker to perform it.

A religion may command its adherents to groom themselves in a
certain way (for example, men may not shave their beards) or to wear
certain clothing (for example, head coverings). Most employers can accommodate to such practices without difficulty. If the practices interfere
with safety on the job, however, or compromise a uniform that serves a
business purpose, employers need not permit them.

A labor union may not try to stop an employer from making reasonable accommodation, and a union must accommodate to the religious observances of its members. A vexing problem over the years has
been dues. Some religions forbid their adherents from joining unions or
paying dues to them, yet many collective bargaining agreements contain
union security clauses that require workers to join or pay dues to a
union. In the past, the courts held that unions had the right to require
employers to discharge religious objectors who refused to pay their dues.
Many generous unions waived this right, however, and customarily per-

mitted religious objectors to pay the equivalent of dues to a charity. The union gave up its dues, but the worker was in a sense paying for the value of union representation. In 1980, section 19 of the National Labor Relations Act was amended to make this custom a legal requirement.

Retaliation

Title VII contains a fourth definition of discrimination, namely, "retaliation." This definition differs from the other three in that it protects, not characteristics of workers like race or sex, but certain acts performed by workers. Two kinds of act are protected: participating in an investigation or a hearing about discrimination and directly opposing discrimination. Illegal retaliation by an employer includes discharge, demotion, transfer, harassment, and supplying an unfavorable recommendation to another employer. Illegal retaliation by a union includes fines, expulsion, and refusal to process a grievance because a charge of discrimination is pending with the government.

Participation in a Hearing or an Investigation

A worker may participate in an investigation or a hearing in various ways. For example, a worker may file a charge with a state fair employment practices agency or with the federal Equal Employment Opportunity Commission. A worker may also provide evidence during a state or federal investigation or give testimony during a hearing or trial. A worker who does any of these things is protected against two adverse actions: the employer may not retaliate against the worker on the job, and (except in an unusual case) the employer may not sue the worker for defamation of business.

Retaliation on the Job Participation is fully protected against retaliation on the job. An employer may do nothing adversely to affect the employment status of a worker because that worker has participated in an investigation or a hearing about discrimination. The reason is that the law against discrimination could not be enforced if workers feared retaliation. It is so important for workers to feel free to participate that this protection applies even if the worker knowingly files a false charge or gives false evidence. (Of course, it is a crime to do such things, and a worker might be prosecuted by the government for them. Nonetheless, an employer may not retaliate on the job.)

Lawsuit for Defamation of a Business   When a worker's words injure an employer's business, two legitimate interests come into conflict. On the one side is the employer, who has suffered a loss and wants to sue for defamation of business to recoup the loss. On the other side is the public policy of eliminating discrimination, which requires that workers come forward with their evidence. These two interests are accommodated by the following rules.

(1) Statements in court. An employer may not sue a worker for defamation based on the worker's testimony during a hearing or a trial—even if the worker knowingly gives false testimony.

(2) Statements out of court. An employer may not sue a worker for defamation based on out-of-court participation, such as filing a charge or giving evidence to investigators, as long as the worker acts in good faith. But an employer may sue if the worker either knows the out-of-court statement is false or, knowing it might be false, recklessly makes it without checking on it.

Directly Opposing Discrimination

In addition to protecting workers who participate in investigations and hearings about discrimination, Title VII protects workers who directly oppose discrimination. An employer may not retaliate against a worker because the worker has opposed this or another employer's discriminatory acts. Thus, an employer may not discharge or refuse to hire a "troublemaker." For example, suppose a worker believes that a supervisor has discriminated against women or people of color in making recommendations for promotion, and the worker complains to the director of personnel. The company may not discipline the worker for making the complaint. Congress created this protection because workers' opposition to discrimination can contribute to the national goal of eradicating racist and sexist employment practices. If Congress had not created this protection, the director of personnel in the foregoing example might never learn about the supervisor's discriminatory behavior.

Direct opposition may take various forms. Protests within the company are protected, for example, speaking to managers and circulating a petition among co-workers. Public opposition is also protected, including making statements to news media and civil rights organizations.

To benefit from the protection against retaliation, a worker's opposition to discrimination must be reasonable in two ways. First, the worker must have a reasonable belief that the employer is violating the law. Holding a reasonable belief is not the same as being right. Workers know that they are not experts and that they sometimes have mistaken impressions about the facts of a case or about the law. If opposition were protected only if the worker is right, workers would often hesitate to oppose discrimination out of fear of retaliation. Accordingly, opposition to discrimination is protected as long as the worker believes in good faith, based on evidence, that the employer is violating Title VII.

Second, a worker's opposition to discrimination must be expressed in a reasonable way. Illegal acts, though undertaken to oppose discrimination, are not protected. Thus, a worker is not privileged to punch a discriminatory supervisor in the nose or to blow up the plant. Opposition is not protected if it interferes with performance on the job. A worker may not refuse to perform normal duties during working hours, even if the time is used to oppose discrimination (for example, by talking to coworkers); however, striking and boycotting to oppose discrimination are protected.

True statements are protected, even if they damage the business. Thus, if a worker truthfully informs the news media about the employer's discriminatory acts, the employer may not retaliate. False statements are also protected if they are made in good faith and are based on reasonable evidence; but false statements are not protected if the worker either knows they are false or, knowing they might be false, recklessly makes them without verifying them first.

A common issue is the use of angry language. On the one hand, discrimination is an emotional issue, and a worker should not lose protection merely for using strong words. On the other hand, even justified anger can get out of control and become insubordinate. The line is hard to draw between strong words and insubordination, and a worker who is opposing discrimination is advised to speak as moderately as possible.

Finally, a worker may oppose discrimination against others. Men are protected in opposing discrimination against women. European-Americans are protected in opposing discrimination against people of color. Indeed, workers are protected in opposing discrimination against customers.

Remedies

Courts have the power to issue injunctions in Title VII cases. Therefore, an employer, union, or employment agency can be ordered to stop committing a discriminatory act. For example, a court might order an employer to cease using an invalid test that has a disparate impact. If the victim of discrimination was denied a job or discharged, the court can order that the victim be hired or reinstated with back seniority.

In addition, courts can award back pay. If the victim has lost wages, the court will order the defendant to pay the victim the wages that the victim would have earned. If contributions would have been made to a pension plan on behalf of the victim, the employer may be ordered to make those contributions as well.

In two situations, a victim of discrimination who has lost wages might not receive back pay. The first situation is the case in which the victim was not available for work. The law requires a victim to participate actively in the labor market. One may not retire and expect to receive a bonanza when one's lawsuit is won. Indeed, if one stops working or searching for work for any reason, even if one is sick and unable to work, money that could reasonably have been earned during this time will be deducted from one's recovery. If one finds another job, money actually earned will also be deducted.

The second situation in which a victim of discrimination might not receive back pay is the case of mixed motives. In an example given above, an employer said, "I did not promote Black because she was frequently absent from work and because she is an African-American." In the past, the courts held that the employer had not broken the law if the legal reason was strong enough by itself to have motivated the decision. Thus, if the employer proved that anyone with Black's absences would not have been promoted, the court would have held for the employer. But if the court found that the illegal reason—Black's race—was necessary to the employer's decision, the court would have held for the plaintiff. Congress changed this rule in 1991, but only in part. As we noted above, Title VII now says that, if any part of an employer's motivation is illegal, the resulting act is discriminatory. A court may issue an injunction against the employer and award attorney's fees to the plaintiff.

Some of the old rule has survived, however. A court must deny back pay if it finds that the legal reason was strong enough by itself to have motivated the decision. The theory seems to be that an employer should not be influenced by illegal reasons, but a worker who has not been harmed by an illegal reason should not receive a lucky benefit. Black would not deserve back pay if her absenteeism, not her race, blocked her promotion.

Victims of intentional discrimination (disparate treatment and retaliation, but *not* disparate impact or failure to make reasonable accommodation) can also recover money as compensation for economic losses and emotional distress. Suppose Berdovitz is discharged because of his national origin, and he cannot find another job for six months. If during this time his car is repossessed because he cannot make the payments, his credit rating is damaged, and he is emotionally distraught because of the humiliation of all that had happened to him, he can recover money as compensation for these losses. And, if the employer's behavior was malicious, punitive damages may be awarded.

Finally, a victim of discrimination is entitled to a reasonable attorney's fee. In some cases, this fee can exceed the amount of money the employer must pay to the victim.

Procedures for Bringing a Claim under Title VII

Title VII allows victims of discrimination to bring lawsuits in federal court. Congress believed, however, that many claims of discrimination can be settled out of court through negotiations and conciliation. To promote settlement, the statute provides that a lawsuit cannot be filed until at least one administrative agency has had an opportunity to investigate the claim and to attempt to resolve it. The federal agency with this responsibility is the Equal Employment Opportunity Commission (EEOC). Many city and state governments have similar agencies, for example, the Fair Employment Practices Commission in California and the Division of Human Rights in New York.

Congress also believed that local matters should be handled locally whenever possible. Consequently, Title VII provides that, if there is a city or state agency ("local agency") that deals with employment discrimination, the local agency must be given a chance to work on a claim before it may be brought to the EEOC. Not all states have such agencies, however. Also, some local agencies have less jurisdiction than the EEOC. For example, the law of Georgia prohibits race and sex discrimination by the state government but not by private employers. Therefore, the local agency in Georgia has no jurisdiction to investigate a charge against a private employer, and it would make no sense to require a person with a charge against a private employer to go to the Georgia agency. As a result, the procedures for filing a Title VII claim vary according to whether there is a local antidiscrimination agency with jurisdiction over the charge.

Before examining the specific procedures for bringing a Title VII claim, we must define a few terms. A "charge" is a statement of the facts that show discrimination has occurred. A charge must be written, signed, and filed with a local agency or with the EEOC. A "charging party" is someone who files a charge of discrimination. Anyone may be a charging party. Usually, it is the person who believes oneself to be a victim of discrimination, but it can also be another person who files the charge on behalf of the victim, for example, a friend. A "respondent" is an employer, union, or employment agency that is accused of discriminatory behavior. If the case goes to court, the respondent becomes the defendant in the lawsuit.

Procedures in Places That Have Antidiscrimination Agencies

If discrimination occurs in a place that has a local agency that deals with the kind of discrimination the victim has suffered, the charging party must file a charge with the local agency before going to the EEOC. After the local agency closes the case, a charge must be filed with the EEOC. But often local agencies are unable to handle cases quickly. Congress decided that sixty days was a reasonable period for a local agency to work on a case. If the local agency has not closed the case within sixty days, the charging party may then file a charge with the EEOC. (A charging party often goes directly to the EEOC, but it cannot accept the charge yet. Usually, the EEOC files the charge with the local agency on behalf of the charging party and sixty days later accepts the charge.)

Title VII contains a number of very short "statutes of limitations." The first requires that, in a state with a local agency, a charge must be filed with the EEOC within three hundred days of the act of discrimination. This period includes the sixty days during which a local agency can work on the case. Thus, suppose an employer refuses to hire a worker on March 2. The last day for filing a charge with the EEOC will be three hundred days later, December 27. Because the local agency can take up to sixty days to work on the case, the local charge should be filed by October 28. (If the charging party files the local charge less than sixty days before the EEOC charge must be filed, for example, on November 5, one may ask the local agency to close the case quickly so that a charge can be filed with the EEOC on time.)

When a charge is filed with the EEOC, it is supposed to investigate the facts and reach a conclusion about whether or not discrimination has occurred. There are two reasons that the EEOC may find that discrimination has not occurred. First, the facts in the charge may be false. For example, suppose the charge alleges that the respondent, a union, refused to admit the charging party because of her sex, but the investigation reveals that she was actually denied membership because she refused to take the oath of allegiance. Second, the facts in the charge may be true, but they do not reveal a violation of Title VII. For example, suppose the charge alleges that an employer fired the charging party because she contributed to the Democratic party. Perhaps it is unjust for an employer to discriminate against a person because of political beliefs, but Title VII does not prohibit such behavior.

If the EEOC decides, for either of these reasons, that discrimination has not occurred, the EEOC closes its file and issues a "right-to-sue" letter. Even though the victim of discrimination has "lost" in the EEOC, one may still file a lawsuit. One must act speedily: the suit must be filed within ninety days of receiving the right-to-sue letter. This is an exceptionally short statute of limitations, and a victim of discrimination must act promptly to find a lawyer. (If one cannot find a lawyer and the ninety days is running out, one may ask the EEOC for help.)

The preceding paragraph discussed what happens when the EEOC concludes that discrimination did not occur. Now let us consider what happens when the EEOC concludes that discrimination probably did occur. First comes conciliation. The EEOC tries to persuade the respondent to cease discriminating and to compensate the victim for losses caused by the discrimination; the EEOC may also ask the victim to make some concessions. If conciliation is successful, the charging party, the respondent, and the EEOC sign a settlement agreement in which the charging party gives up the right to sue and the respondent promises to do whatever was agreed upon, for example, pay money or reinstate the victim to a job.

If conciliation fails, the EEOC must make a decision. Title VII empowers the EEOC to file lawsuits on behalf of victims of discrimination, but Congress never gives the EEOC a budget large enough for it to sue on every valid claim. As a rule, the EEOC sues only when an important issue of law is involved or when the respondent has discriminated against large numbers of persons. In the rare case in which the EEOC decides to sue, the victim need do nothing further (though one may hire one's own lawyer and participate in the case). In the usual case in which the EEOC decides not to sue, it closes its file and issues a right-to-sue letter. One must file a lawsuit within ninety days of receiving this letter.

The reader may have noticed several paragraphs back the statement that the EEOC "is supposed to" investigate the facts of a charge and determine whether discrimination has occurred. These words were deliberately chosen because the EEOC receives such a large number of charges that many receive little or no attention. Curiously, there is no limit in Title VII on how long the EEOC may hold a case. It is possible that a charge might not be investigated until years after it was filed, and the

EEOC might not sue, or issue a right-to-sue letter, for another period of years. If so much time passes that the defendant in the lawsuit cannot defend the case adequately, the court may allow a motion to dismiss the case. Also, a victim of discrimination may not wish to wait years for the EEOC to deal with the case. Accordingly, Title VII provides that, if the EEOC has not closed a case within 180 days after the charge was filed, the victim may request a right-to-sue letter. The EEOC will issue the letter, and the victim may file a lawsuit within 90 days of receiving the letter. Also, if a victim wishes to sue at once, without waiting 180 days (for example, one might be suffering serious losses that cannot be compensated for in the future), the EEOC will usually close a case at once and issue a right-to-sue letter.

Procedures in Places That Lack Antidiscrimination Agencies

If discrimination occurs in a place that does not have a local agency that deals with the kind of discrimination the victim has suffered, the charging party must file a charge with the EEOC within 180 days of the act of discrimination. Assuming the charge is filed on time, the rules of law and the EEOC procedures are identical to the rules and procedures discussed above for cases that occurred in places that have antidiscrimination agencies.

2
The Age Discrimination in Employment Act

The Age Discrimination in Employment Act of 1967 does for older workers what Title VII does for women and people of color. This chapter explains who is protected by the Age Act and who must obey it, what is prohibited by the act, the remedies it authorizes, and the procedures for bringing a claim.

Who Is Protected by the Age Act

The Age Act prohibits age discrimination against any worker aged forty or older. A worker is not protected by this law until the worker is at least forty. Therefore, an employer does not violate the Age Act by denying a job to a twenty-five-year-old on the ground that the person is too young. (The employer might be violating a local law, however; and if the employer is an agency of government, the employer might also be violating the Constitution.)

For many years, the Age Act also contained a maximum age; when workers reached this maximum, they lost the protection of the act. A worker who was over the maximum age could be discharged, denied employment, or discriminated against in any other way because of age. From 1967 to 1978, the maximum age was sixty-five, and from 1978 to 1986 the maximum age was seventy. Since 1987, however, the maximum age has been removed from the act. Today, with a few exceptions, all workers are protected against age discrimination from age forty until death.

One exception in the Age Act applies to the jobs of police officer and fire fighter in state and local governments. The government may refuse to hire an applicant for these jobs who is over a certain age, and it may force an officer or fire fighter who reaches a certain age to retire. The reason for this exception is the strong correlation between advanced age and inability to perform these jobs. Another exception allows a college to retire a tenured professor at age seventy. The reason for this exception is the great difficulty of discharging tenured professors for unsatisfactory performance; without a fixed retirement age, they might keep their jobs although their effectiveness as teachers and scholars had diminished. Both of these exceptions expire at the end of 1993, however, and it is uncertain whether Congress will renew them.

The Age Act also protects United States citizens employed by United States businesses operating in foreign countries.

Who Must Obey the Age Act

The Age Act covers private employers with twenty or more workers, state and local governments, and employment agencies. The Age Act also covers labor unions that have twenty-five or more members or that operate a hiring hall that supplies workers to a covered employer. The Age Act does not cover apprenticeship programs, which are specifically designed for young people preparing to enter the labor market. Religious organizations are treated like any other private employers, so they are covered if they have twenty or more employees; however, constitutional protection for freedom of religion means that the relationship of minister to church is not covered by the act.

The Age Act permits state and local government to provide greater protections than federal law does. As a result, a city or state may protect workers who are not covered by the federal law. For example, New York's law protects workers aged eighteen and older. But any state or local law that is inconsistent with the Age Act (for example, a law requiring all city employees to retire at age sixty-five) is invalid.

Disparate Treatment

The Age Act prohibits discrimination in the same words as Title VII does. Consequently, courts interpreting the Age Act have borrowed three of Title VII's definitions of discrimination—disparate treatment, disparate impact, and retaliation. (Title VII's fourth definition of discrimination, reasonable accommodation, applies to religious discrimination only and is not part of the Age Act.)

Disparate treatment under the Age Act means denying an opportunity to a worker, or providing inferior compensation or terms and conditions of employment, because of age. Thus, it is illegal for an employer to set a maximum age for a job (except in a few unusual cases, discussed below, in which age is a bona fide occupational qualification). It is illegal for an employer to compensate an older worker less than a younger worker because of age; compensation includes all kinds of pay—not only salary, but also vacation pay, sick pay, and overtime pay. It is illegal for an employer to deny an older worker an opportunity such as training, a job assignment, or overtime work because of age. It is illegal for an employer to require older workers to pass a physical or mental examination that is not required of younger workers. These rules hold even though an employer's reason for discriminating is an honest belief that older workers are, on the average, more expensive to employ, less productive, or more likely to become ill.

Role of Intent

As we noted in our discussion of Title VII, the key to disparate treatment is intent, and intent sometimes poses difficult questions. For example, is it permissible for an employer who is not prejudiced against older workers to refuse to hire a person over age forty because customers or co-workers prefer a younger person in the job? The answer is no; customers or employees must not be allowed to force an employer to break the law.

An interesting puzzle exists concerning mixed motives in Age Act cases. Before the 1991 amendments, the rules on mixed motives were the same for Title VII and the Age Act. As we noted about Title VII, if an employer had both a legal and an illegal reason for a decision, the employer won the case if the legal reason, by itself, was strong enough to have motivated the decision; the worker won if the illegal reason was necessary to the decision. Curiously, the 1991 amendments changed this rule for Title VII but not for the Age Act. What will the courts do? They might continue to follow the old rule for Age Act cases. Yet it seems more likely that the courts will realize that Congress simply forgot to conform the Age Act to Title VII but surely wanted to; there seems to be no good reason to treat mixed motives one way under the Age Act and a different way under Title VII. If the act is interpreted this way, when an employer's decision is motivated by both a worker's age and a legitimate reason (for example, decreased productivity), the decision is discriminatory, and the court will order the employer not to be influenced by age in the future. The court may order reinstatement and back pay for the worker if age was necessary to the decision; but if age was not necessary—if a legal reason such as decreased productivity was, by itself, sufficient to have motivated the decision—the court may not order reinstatement or award damages.

Examples of Disparate Treatment

Advertisements If an employer may not prefer one age group over another, surely an employer may not advertise a preference for workers of a certain age group. Phrases like "young," "age 25 to 30," "boy," "girl," and "college student" are plainly illegal because they exclude older workers. Phrases like "age 65," "retired person," and "supplement your pension" are also prohibited because they imply that younger protected workers (between, say, ages forty and sixty) are not wanted.

Applications EEOC interpretations of the Age Act disapprove of (but do not prohibit) employment applications that ask for the applicant's date of birth or age. Asking a worker's age often discourages older persons from applying. If age is stated on an application, the employer cannot deny knowing the applicant's age and, therefore, is open to a lawsuit. As a result, an employer should not ask an applicant's age unless there is a genuine need for this information *before* hiring. (*After* hiring, employers may ask a worker's age if the information is necessary for a legitimate reason, for example, a pension plan.)

Fringe Benefits except Pensions Life insurance is more expensive for older workers because they are more likely to die. Likewise, medical insurance is more costly for older workers because they are more likely to contract serious illnesses. Congress understood that these facts present real problems for employers, but Congress also wanted to protect older workers. The following rules are Congress's attempt to balance the interests of employers and older workers. The rules apply only to fringe benefits, not to wages or salary, and they do not apply to pensions (which are discussed below). The rules are based on the principle that benefits may be adjusted so that the costs for younger and older workers are approximately equal.

Before we state these rules, three points should be made. First, benefits do not have to be adjusted. An employer is free to provide the same benefits to older workers as to younger workers. Second, an employer may allow—but may not require—older workers, on an individual basis, to reduce their salaries so they may maintain full benefits; older workers who choose this option must not bear a higher proportion of the total cost of benefit premiums than younger workers do. Third, because an employer is allowed to reduce benefits to equalize costs for younger and older workers, an employer has no good reason—and it is against the law—to refuse to hire or to discharge an older worker on account of the cost of pension or insurance benefits. Along the same lines, some benefits cost the same for younger and older workers, for example, paid vacation and sick days; these benefits may not be reduced because of a worker's age.

A specific benefit may be reduced for older workers because of cost. Thus, because life insurance costs more for older persons, an employer may equalize costs by reducing the death benefit for older workers. An employer need not provide life insurance at all; but if the employer provides life insurance for younger workers, the employer may not totally deny life insurance to workers older than a certain age. The same rule applies to disability and medical benefits.

Instead of reducing one or more specific benefits to allow for the extra cost of older workers, an employer may adjust a package of benefits. The overall reduction, however, must not result in the total cost to the employer being lower or the benefits to workers less favorable than if specific benefits had been reduced. If a reduction in one benefit is greater than a specific-benefits approach would produce, the excess reduction must be offset by an increase in another benefit available to the same workers. Also, a benefits-package approach may not include a pension plan and may not be used to justify greater reductions in medical benefits than a specific-benefits approach would produce. For example, suppose an employer offers benefits X, Y, and Z, none of which is a pension plan, and the cost of each of these benefits is about the same. Suppose also that the extra costs for older workers would justify reducing each benefit by 10 percent. Because of the workers' needs, the employer chooses not to reduce benefit X. The employer may reduce benefits Y and Z by 15 percent, or benefit Y by 20 percent and Z by 10 percent, or any other combination adding up to the same total savings, so long as medical-care benefits are not cut by more than 10 percent.

Layoffs A layoff (or forced retirement) is illegal if it is motivated by a desire to eliminate older workers. Therefore, an employer may not lay off according to age. Nor may an employer use a substitute for age. There are many such substitutes. Some of them are years of service, eligibility for pensions, and "potential." Thus, an employer may not lay off an older worker because a younger one has "a better future" with the company. (Similarly, an employer may not refuse to hire on the basis of a substitute for age.)

Severance Pay Severance pay may be awarded if it is based on factors other than age, such as a percentage of salary (for example, two weeks' pay) or years of service. We noted in the preceding paragraph that factors such as years of service are substitutes for age; nevertheless, they may be used in connection with severance pay because they favor (rather than discriminate against) older workers. Severance pay may not be completely denied to workers who are laid off merely on the ground that they are eligible for pensions; eligibility for pensions is another substitute for age, and it disfavors older workers. Severance pay, however, may be reduced by pension benefits according to a formula in the Age Act.

Retirement Age When the Age Act contained a maximum age, an employer was free to force a worker who reached that age to retire. Some retirement plans specified a normal retirement age that was less than the maximum age in the act; for example, when the act protected workers until age sixty-five, a number of plans provided that workers had to retire at age sixty. The Supreme Court held that these plans were lawful under an exception in the act. Congress subsequently disapproved of this holding and reworded the exception, so workers could not be compelled to retire before reaching the maximum age.

Now that Congress has completely removed the maximum age from the act, a retirement plan may not require a worker to retire, however old the worker may be—assuming, of course, the worker is performing satisfactorily on the job. (A narrow exception exists to this rule: a worker in an executive or high policy-making position may be forced to retire at age sixty-five if the worker is entitled to an annual pension from the employer of at least $44,000.)

Employers occasionally wish to induce workers to retire early and, accordingly, offer added pension and other benefits. Sometimes the added benefits increase according to the worker's age, salary, or seniority. A "golden parachute" is legal if it is offered to all workers, regardless of age (though the minimum retirement age in the pension plan may still be observed) and if workers are not threatened with retaliation if they do not accept the offer.

Some workers who accepted early retirement later sued their employer, claiming they were pressured to accept. To protect against such lawsuits, employers now frequently require a worker accepting early retirement to sign a waiver of the right to sue. Several requirements must be satisfied for such a waiver to be legal. Among them are that the worker must receive extra money or benefits beyond what the worker is already entitled to; the worker must be given time to consider whether to accept and time to back out after accepting; and the waiver must be written understandably, specifically refer to the Age Act, advise the worker to consult a lawyer, and, of course, be truly voluntary.

Pensions Pension plans are more costly for older workers because they are more likely to draw benefits in the near future, yet pensions are especially important to workers as they near retirement. Congress wrote some complicated rules to balance these interests.

Pension plans come in different varieties, but some rules apply to all of them. All plans may adopt a minimum retirement age (for example, fifty). A worker may not retire with benefits before this age, regardless of how long the worker has been employed. All plans may establish a normal retirement age (for example, sixty-five). An employer may stop contributing to the plan when a worker reaches the normal retirement age (though, of course, the worker cannot be forced to retire), and an employer need not contribute for a worker who was older than retirement age when hired. All pension plans may offer workers the opportunity to retire early if they choose. All plans may require early retirement for reasons other than age, for example, total disability.

Other rules for pension plans vary according to the variety of the plan. In a "defined contribution" plan, a specific sum of money (for example, $100 per month) is contributed into a separate pension account and invested on behalf of a worker. When the worker retires, the account is used to buy an annuity (which is usually a fixed benefit paid each month for as long as the worker or the worker's spouse lives). The amount of the retirement benefit depends on the amount in the account; there is no maximum or minimum benefit, and the employer does not guarantee how much the benefit will be. As a result, under a defined contribution plan the cost for an older worker is the same as for a younger worker. Therefore, a worker who is hired before the normal retirement age may not be excluded from a defined contribution plan.

In a "defined benefit" plan, the employer promises to pay a worker a specific monthly benefit on retirement. Commonly, the benefit is determined by a formula that includes years of service and annual salary at retirement, up to a maximum. The employer guarantees payment of the benefit and so must contribute and invest enough money annually to fund the benefits that will be paid in the future. As a result, under a defined benefit plan the cost for an older worker can be higher than for a younger worker. Contributions for older workers are invested for a shorter period of time and earn less interest. Also, some younger workers will leave the company before working five years, when their pensions would vest, and money put aside for them can be used to fund benefits for other workers; but older workers are more likely to keep their jobs until their pensions vest. In addition, some younger workers will stay with the company long enough to receive the maximum benefit, after which time the employer need not make further contributions on their behalf; but few older workers will stay so long. Therefore, a worker hired less than five years before the normal retirement age may be excluded from a defined benefit plan.

Proving Disparate Treatment

The methods for proving intentional age discrimination are the same as the methods for proving intentional race or sex discrimination. The following discussion is limited to special features of proving age discrimination.

Traditional Proof Sometimes an employer's words provide evidence of the intent to discriminate, as when an employer says to a worker, "You are too old for this job." Of course, not every remark about age proves discriminatory intent. It was not discriminatory when an employer mentioned, in passing, that older workers often have problems adjusting to new policies.

Another traditional way to prove disparate treatment is to show that an older worker was denied an opportunity that a younger worker was allowed to take advantage of. An airline allowed pilots who lost their jobs to use their seniority to bid on jobs as flight engineers. But this opportunity was available only to pilots under age sixty; if older pilots lost their jobs, they had to retire. When a pilot named Thurston challenged this policy, the Supreme Court ruled against the airline because it afforded an opportunity to younger workers but denied it to older ones.

The *McDonnell Douglas* formula is readily adaptable to age cases. Thus, an inference of intent arises if it is proved that the plaintiff is at least forty years old, applied for a vacant position, was qualified and was rejected, and the employer continued to accept applications or hired a substantially younger person.

An employer may rebut traditional proof of discrimination by showing the plaintiff's evidence is false or by presenting evidence of a legitimate reason for the action. For example, an employer might testify that the plaintiff was rejected, not because of age, but because of lack of skill. Of course, it would not suffice for an employer to testify that the plaintiff was rejected because of a substitute for age such as lack of potential, or for an illegal reason such as the increased cost of insurance.

Occasionally, when charged with *race* or *sex* discrimination, an employer can defend the case by proving that a person of the same race or sex as the plaintiff was awarded the employment opportunity. For example, suppose an African-American named Brown applies for a job, is not hired, and accuses the employer of race discrimination. The employer proves that the job went to Coffey, who is also an African-American. This proof goes a long way toward defeating Brown's case because, if an employer hires one African-American for a job, it is unlikely that the employer rejected another African-American because of race. (This proof is not conclusive, however, because an employer might illegally insist that African-Americans have higher qualifications than European-Americans. If a European-American with Brown's qualifications had been hired, the employer would have discriminated against Brown.)

This kind of proof also works in *age* cases—but only if the hired worker is older than the rejected one. Thus, suppose an employer replaces a fifty-year-old person with a sixty-year-old. It is unlikely that this employer is discriminating because of age. But suppose the employer replaces the fifty-year-old with a forty-year-old. Even though both of these workers are in the class protected by the Age Act, these facts tend to prove age discrimination.

Statistical Proof Statistics may be used to prove intent to discriminate under the Age Act in the same way as they may under Title VII. If in a year two thousand workers, half of whom are aged forty or older, apply for one thousand jobs as clerks in a chain of department stores, and eight hundred of the younger but only two hundred of the older applicants are hired, it is very unlikely that this outcome occurred by chance, and age was probably a cause. But age is often associated with legitimate explanations; therefore, statistical proof of age discrimination requires even more precision than statistical proof of race or sex discrimination. The Supreme Court was convinced by evidence in the truck drivers' case (see pp. 11–12) that people of color held less than 1 percent of the line driving jobs in communities in which people of color were one-third of the population. Suppose it had been an age case. The Court might not have been convinced by proof that older workers held 1 percent of line driving jobs in communities in which older people were one-third of the population; the reason is the strong possibility of a legitimate explanation, for example, that older workers are less interested than younger ones in driving trucks across the country.

Defenses for Disparate Treatment

The Age Act allows an employer to treat older workers differently from younger workers when age is a bona fide occupational qualification (bfoq) for a job or when the employer acts on the basis of a factor other than age.

Bona Fide Occupational Qualification Employers sometimes wish to prevent workers over a designated age from performing certain work. A bus company might refuse to hire drivers over a certain age; an airline might wish to retire pilots when they become older. The employers' reason is the belief that older workers are not able to perform the work satisfactorily. Congress recognized that this reason can be legitimate in some cases. The Age Act states that age is a bfoq for a job when a decision based on age is "reasonably necessary to the normal operation" of a business.

In another case against an airline, a valid federal regulation required that commercial pilots and co-pilots retire at age sixty. The regulation did not apply to flight engineers. Nonetheless, the airline required its flight engineers to retire at sixty because they might have to take over the controls in an emergency. A flight engineer named Criswell sued under the Age Act. In defense, the airline argued that being less than sixty was a bfoq for the job. The Supreme Court held that age can be a bfoq only on condition that (1) all or almost all workers over the designated age are unable to perform the essential duties of the job in a safe and efficient manner, or (2) some workers over the designated age possess a physical trait that prevents them from performing safely and efficiently, and the trait cannot be detected on an individual basis. The Court sustained a jury verdict for the flight engineer because the airline failed to prove either of these conditions.

In deciding whether age is a bfoq for a job, economic factors such as the increased cost of training older workers or their supposed lower productivity are not relevant; rather, the health and safety of customers and co-workers are crucial. The more likely that harm would occur, and the more serious the harm would be, the more willing a court is to recognize age as a bfoq. Thus, safety concerns allowed a bus company to hire only drivers who were under thirty-five. The union contract assigned newly hired drivers to charters, which are very demanding; and it took drivers about ten years to earn the seniority to claim a regular route. Therefore, if older drivers had been hired, they would have had to make difficult charter trips during their declining years. The ability safely to drive a bus deteriorates with age, but medical examinations of individuals cannot reveal which ones are at risk. Based on these facts, the court upheld age as a bfoq.

Factors Other Than Age An employer may base an employment decision on a factor other than age (assuming the factor does not have a disparate impact, which is discussed below). Naturally, qualification for the job and performance on the job are factors other than age; so an employer may hire a thirty-five-year-old instead of a forty-two-year-old because the younger person is better qualified, and an employer may lay off a forty-two-year-old instead of a thirty-five-year-old because the older person is less productive. (In both cases, the employer is well advised to have objective evidence, rather than mere opinion, as to the workers' qualifications or productivity.)

Being "overqualified" for a job is not a factor other than age. Too much experience or education is directly related to age, is not related to job performance, and disqualifies older workers. Having the most experience is a legitimate factor, however, because it relates to job performance and does not tend to eliminate older workers.

Market forces are a factor other than age. To attract qualified new workers, who tend to be young, an employer may need to pay them more than present workers, who tend to be older and are doing the same work.

Disparate Impact

Disparate impact refers to a practice that, although not intended to discriminate, has a disproportional adverse effect on older workers and is not justified by the needs of the business. For example, younger workers might pass a physical test given to applicants at a much higher rate than older workers. Unless it is a business necessity, the test is illegal.

Proving Disparate Impact

The rules that govern disparate impact need not be restated because they are almost the same as under Title VII. One difference, however, is that under the Age Act a disparate impact must apply to the entire class of workers over forty; a disparate impact on some workers over forty (for example, those over sixty) is not illegal.

Business Necessity

If the plaintiffs establish a disparate impact, the employer may defend on the ground that the practice is necessary to the business. Again, the rules are the same as under Title VII. For example, a selection device such as a written or physical test that has a disparate impact on older workers is legal if the test can be validated (that is, if the test predicts success on the job).

Does saving money qualify as a business necessity? The answer is usually no. Thus, a school district that wanted to economize adopted a policy of hiring only teachers with less than five years of experience. The policy had a disparate impact on older workers because the policy disqualified more than 90 percent of teachers over forty, as compared to about 60 percent of teachers under forty. The district argued that saving money is a business necessity; but the court held that saving money is not related to successful job performance, and age discrimination cannot be justified on economic grounds.

In an extreme situation, however, saving money can be a business necessity. Suppose a company on the verge of bankruptcy decides to lay off its highest paid employees. Compensation is associated with age, so the company's decision has a disparate impact on older employees. If cost reduction is unavoidable, it is a business necessity; and if the layoffs are the least detrimental alternative for reducing costs, they are permissible.

Seniority

Like Title VII, the Age Act protects seniority systems that were created and are administered in good faith. Normally, seniority operates in favor of older workers and raises no problems under the Age Act. Thus, employers need not worry about laying off junior workers before senior workers, and union hiring halls need not worry about referring workers in order of seniority. Yet it is possible that, in a specific case, seniority would favor younger workers. For example, suppose an employer's work force has traditionally been composed of younger workers, but recently older workers have been hired. If layoffs become necessary and seniority is observed, the older workers will be the first to go. Even in this case, however, observing seniority would not violate the Age Act as long as the seniority system was not created or administered for the purpose of putting older workers at a disadvantage.

"Reverse seniority" means giving the advantage to the worker with less, rather than more, time with the company. Reverse seniority is not protected by the Age Act. Therefore, if reverse seniority has an adverse effect on older workers (as will almost always be true), the employer must show that the practice is necessary to the business.

Retaliation

The Age Act prohibits retaliation against a worker who opposes age discrimination or who participates in an investigation or trial of age discrimination. The Age Act is identical to Title VII in this regard.

Procedures and Remedies

The procedures for enforcing the Age Act are similar to those under Title VII. In a state that has no local agency that deals with age discrimination, a charge must be filed with the EEOC within 180 days of the discriminatory action. In a state that has a local agency, charges must be filed with both the local agency and the EEOC (but, unlike Title VII, under the Age Act either charge may be filed first); the EEOC charge must be filed within 300 days of the discriminatory action or within 30 days after the local agency completes its work. In all states, the EEOC, when it finishes working on a charge, will issue a right-to-sue letter. A lawsuit must be filed within 90 days after this letter is received.

Some of the remedies in the Age Act are similar to the remedies under Title VII. Back pay, injunctions, and attorney's fees are governed by the same principles under the two statutes.

Other remedies under the Age Act are different from Title VII. The Age Act does not allow compensatory damages for economic losses or punitive damages. The Age Act does, however, permit a court to award "liquidated damages," which is a sum of money awarded in addition to back pay. Liquidated damages may be as little as $1 or as much as the total back pay awarded. Liquidated damages are appropriate only if the employer willfully violated the act, that is, knew the act applied and deliberately disregarded it. A judge may reduce or deny liquidated damages if the employer acted reasonably and in good faith.

3
Title I of the Americans with Disabilities Act

Title I of the Americans with Disabilities Act of 1990 applies to employment. The Disability Act prohibits discrimination against qualified workers with disabilities (in the past, we used the word "handicaps") and requires employers to make reasonable accommodation to workers' known disabilities unless accommodation would result in undue hardship to the business. The procedures and remedies of the Disability Act are patterned after Title VII.

Because the Disability Act is so new, many issues had not been decided when this bulletin went to press. Guidance can be drawn from committee reports in the House of Representatives and the Senate, from the EEOC regulations, and from the Vocational Rehabilitation Act, which was the cornerstone for the Disability Act. Nonetheless, any rule we draw from these sources must be considered tentative until it has been approved in court. In some instances, not even a tentative rule can be found, and the best we can do is indicate that a question exists and suggest how it might be answered.

Who Must Obey the Disability Act

The Disability Act covers private employers if they have twenty-five or more employees; as of July 26, 1994, this number is reduced to fifteen employees. The act also covers labor unions, employment agencies, and state and local governments. The act does not cover tax-exempt private membership clubs or the United States government.

The Disability Act covers religious associations and societies that have the required number of employees. Although these organizations may give preference to members of their own religion, they may not discriminate against disabled persons.

An employer may not avoid complying with the Disability Act by contracting with another business for employment functions. For example, suppose company C and company T, which are separate firms, make a contract for T to train C's workers. T's facilities are not accessible to people in wheelchairs. C may not refuse to hire or provide training for a worker who uses a wheelchair on the ground that T's facilities are not accessible; rather, C is obligated to ensure that T's facilities are accessible or to choose another company to provide training. Suppose C decides to hold a conference (or a meeting or a party) and wishes to use a hotel. C must ensure that the hotel is accessible to any of C's workers who are eligible to attend the conference.

The Disability Act permits state and local governments to provide additional protections for disabled persons. For example, in Illinois employers of four or more employees are prohibited from discriminating against the disabled.

Who Is Protected by the Disability Act

The Disability Act protects every qualified individual with a disability from employment discrimination. To understand the nature of this protection, the words "disability" and "qualified" must be defined with care.

The Meaning of "Disability"

The law defines the word "disability" broadly. It includes

• a physical or mental impairment that substantially limits one or more of an individual's major life activities, or

• a record of having such an impairment, or

• being regarded as having such an impairment.

Thus, to explain the meaning of "disability," we must first define the meanings of "impairment," "substantially limits," and "major life activities."

Impairment An impairment is a physical or mental condition that restricts one's ability to do what an average person can do. An impairment may be a physical condition such as a missing limb, a mental condition such as a learning disability, or a disease such as emphysema.

Not every condition that might interfere with life amounts to an impairment under the Disability Act. Normal (though somewhat unusual) characteristics are not impairments, for instance, being left-handed. Thus, a left-handed person who could not operate a machine designed for right-handed operators did not have an impairment. Temporary conditions such as a broken arm are not impairments. Neither are behavioral disorders such as compulsive gambling or sexual characteristics such as homosexuality. Having a prison record is not an impairment. An employer who denies employment opportunities to workers on the basis of these conditions does not violate the Disability Act.

Major Life Activities The Disability Act does not define major life activity, but the term seems to refer to the important things that most people can do. Committee reports in Congress gave the examples of caring for oneself, performing manual tasks, hearing, speaking, seeing, walking, learning, breathing, participating in community activities, and, of course, working.

Substantial Limitation To qualify as a disability, an impairment must be a substantial limitation on a major life activity. A minor limitation is not enough. For example, suppose a librarian needs eyeglasses to see normally. Seeing is a major life activity, yet this worker's impairment does not amount to a substantial limitation. But if the librarian could not see normally even with glasses, the impairment would be a substantial limitation.

A person who cannot see normally is limited in the performance of several life activities, but suppose an impairment affects primarily one major life activity—the ability to work. Is such an impairment a substantial limitation? The answer is, it depends. A range of possibilities exists. At one end of the range is an impairment that interferes with one's ability to perform one specific job or occupation. A baseball pitcher whose arm is injured can no longer pursue a career as a pitcher; yet almost every other job in life is still open to him, so his impairment is not a substantial limitation on his ability to work. A lawyer who is afraid of heights may be unable to work for a firm with offices on the top floor of a skyscraper. Her acrophobia closes one job to her, but does not substantially limit her ability to work because there are many other jobs for lawyers in offices at lower heights.

At the other end of the range is an impairment that interferes with one's ability to perform many jobs, for example, an unskilled laborer's back condition that prevents him from lifting heavy weights. Taking into account his education, experience, and so on, this impairment is plainly a substantial limitation on his ability to work.

Cases falling between the extremes of this range are more troublesome. The following criteria, used to decide a similar issue under the Rehabilitation Act, may be helpful in establishing whether an impairment is a substantial limitation on the ability to work: the worker's training and expectations, the number and types of jobs from which the worker is disqualified, and the geographical area to which the worker has reasonable access. In other words, along the range of possibilities, the closer an impairment is to a laborer's bad back, and the further from the pitcher's sore arm and the lawyer's fear of heights, the more likely that the impairment substantially limits the major life activity of working.

The Three Definitions of "Disability" With these definitions in mind, we can understand the three definitions of "disability" in the Disability Act:

(1) An impairment that substantially limits a major life activity is a disability. An example is deafness.

(2) A record of having a disability is a disability. For instance, suppose a worker has been cured of cancer, but she is denied a job for which she is qualified because of this medical history. She has a disability within the meaning of the law, and the employer has discriminated against her.

(3) Being regarded as having a disability is a disability, whether or not one is actually impaired. An example of a worker who has no true impairment is an accountant whose face is disfigured in an accident. Because she is disfigured, she is discharged from her firm. She may in fact be able to do everything she used to do, but her firm regards her as being impaired; for this reason, she has a disability, and her discharge is discriminatory. Another example is a worker who is fired because of a false rumor that he has AIDS or a false belief that he uses illegal drugs.

Status of Contagious Diseases Contagious diseases such as tuberculosis and AIDS (including HIV infection) are impairments. An employer may not discriminate against persons with contagious diseases unless they create a significant risk to the health or safety of other people and the risk cannot be eliminated by reasonable accommodation.

Exclusion for Use of Illegal Drugs A person currently using illegal drugs is not protected by the Disability Act. If an employer provides medical benefits to workers, however, an employee discovered to be using illegal drugs may not be denied medical services. A person who *formerly* used drugs, but who has been or is presently being rehabilitated, is protected; so are people mistakenly believed to be using drugs.

Alcohol and Other Legal Drugs Individuals disabled by alcohol or other legal drugs are protected. Nonetheless, an employer may prohibit the use of alcohol or illegal drugs in the workplace and may prohibit workers from being under their influence at work. An employer may also hold drug users and alcoholics to the same performance standards as other workers.

The Meaning of "Qualified"

A worker with a disability is qualified for a job if the worker meets job-related selection criteria and can perform the essential functions of the job with or without reasonable accommodation. The meaning of "reasonable accommodation" will be discussed below. Here we focus on the other elements of this standard.

Job-Related Selection Criteria Applicants for jobs often have to meet specific selection criteria such as education, experience, or level of skill. A person with a disability should be treated like any other person with respect to such criteria. Thus, if a medical group requires that in-coming doctors have graduated from medical school and successfully completed an internship and a residency, a person in a wheelchair who has not completed a residency is not qualified. But if a person in a wheel-chair meets the criteria—has graduated from medical school and completed an internship and a residency—the person is qualified, and the medical group must make reasonable accommodation to the person's disability.

Essential Functions of the Job Every job has some functions that are essential and some that are marginal. A function is essential if the job exists to perform that function or if only a few workers are available to perform it. For a secretary, typing and answering the telephone are essential functions; moving furniture and buying birthday gifts for the boss's children are marginal. The Disability Act considers a person to be qualified if the person can perform the essential functions. Therefore, suppose a woman applies for the job of secretary in an office. She has a disability that limits her ability to walk. The employer refuses to hire her, saying, "She will not be able to run errands for me." If the job requires running errands daily, she is indeed not qualified. But if running errands is required once or twice a year and other workers can do it, the woman is qualified and the employer has discriminated against her.

Threat to Persons or Property If a worker's disability creates a substantial threat to property or to the health or safety of other persons, and reasonable accommodation cannot eliminate the threat, the worker is not qualified for the job. A person with a highly contagious disease such as hepatitis is not qualified for a job cooking or serving food. But generalizations, irrational fears, or ignorance may not be the basis for determining that a threat exists; rather, a specific and significant risk must be identified, and it must be associated with this particular worker. An employer may not refuse to hire an HIV-positive person as a book-keeper out of fear that other workers in the room might somehow contract the virus, nor may an employer refuse to hire mentally retarded persons based on myths about their behavior.

How should we treat a worker who can perform a job but has a disability which (even after reasonable accommodation) creates a threat to that worker alone? The issue is problematic. On the one hand, we want to avoid paternalism: a person with a disability should have the same right as anyone else to decide whether to take a risk. On the other hand, it makes no sense to put a worker in a job in which one is sure to be hurt. Although the courts will have the final word, Congress seems to have resolved the problem by distinguishing between substantial harm that is likely to occur in the near future and harm that might occur in the distant future.

The specific case Congress thought about was an applicant for a construction job who is hired and then sent for a routine medical examination. Although he has no symptoms and can perform all functions of the job, X rays reveal a potential for back trouble in the future. Is this worker qualified for the job? The report of the committee in the House of Representatives said, "if the examining physician found that there was high probability of substantial harm if the candidate performed the particular functions of the job in question, the employer could reject the candidate, unless the employer could make a reasonable accommodation to the candidate's condition that would avert such harm" (H.R. Report no. 101-485, 101st Cong., 2d sess., pt. 2: 73). But the report went on to say:

> A physical or mental employment criterion [such as passing a medical examination] can be used to disqualify a person with a disability only if [it] has a direct impact on the ability of the person to do their actual job duties without *imminent*, substantial threat of harm (p. 74; emphasis added).

The report used the words "imminent" and "substantial" twice more in the same context. Thus, Congress felt that a person who, despite reasonable accommodation, is likely to hurt oneself seriously in the near future is not qualified, but a worker who might injure oneself in the distant future is qualified. Based on this analysis, the construction worker whose X ray reveals a potential for back trouble in the future should be considered qualified.

It is unclear whether the EEOC accepts this analysis. The EEOC agrees that a worker whose disability creates an imminent and substantial risk to the worker is not qualified; the regulations give the example of a worker who seeks a job using dangerous equipment such as a power saw but who has narcolepsy and can lose consciousness unexpectedly. But the EEOC may not agree about the worker who, though currently able to perform safely, might be injured in the future. The regulations say that the definition of "impairment" does not include "characteristic predisposition to illness or disease." Probably the EEOC intends to authorize the new genetic tests, which seek to determine whether a worker is especially vulnerable to toxic chemicals. But a weakness in the back seems analogous to a weakness in the genes, so perhaps the EEOC, which avoided discussing the case on which Congress focused, thinks the construction worker should not be considered qualified.

Reasonable Accommodation and Undue Hardship

Like Title VII, the Disability Act prohibits discrimination against qualified workers with disabilities. Also like Title VII, the Disability Act does not guarantee equal success, require preferences, or establish quotas for the disabled. But unlike Title VII, which envisions a workplace in which race and sex are ignored, the Disability Act requires that disabilities be recognized and that barriers to employment of the disabled be removed whenever feasible. A disabled worker is qualified if, *with or without* reasonable accommodation, the worker can perform the essential functions of the job.

Sometimes a disability is not a barrier to a job; the worker is fully qualified regardless of the disability. Think of a gardener who is hard of hearing or an artist who uses a wheelchair. In cases like these, the employer's obligation is simply not to discriminate against the disabled worker.

At other times, a disability is a barrier to a job, but measures can be taken to overcome it. A large-print monitor may accommodate a visually impaired worker; a ramp may accommodate a worker in a wheelchair.

The Disability Act does not require an employer to reduce standards of job performance, but the act does require an employer to help a worker with a disability to overcome barriers and meet the standards. Indeed, the act considers a worker to be qualified for a job (and, therefore, protected from discrimination) if the worker can perform the essential functions of the job after the employer has made reasonable accommodation to the worker's disability. Nonetheless, an employer need not undertake an accommodation that would impose an undue hardship on the business.

Reasonable Accommodation   Reasonable accommodations fall into three categories. In the first category are modifications in the job application process that enable a worker with a disability to be considered, for example, providing a large-print version of a written test for a visually impaired applicant. In the second category are modifications to the work environment that enable a worker with a disability to perform the essential functions of the job, for example, supplying a page turner for a worker who cannot use one's hands. In the third category are modifications that allow a worker with a disability to enjoy the same benefits that other workers enjoy, for example, holding a training program or a holiday party in a room that is accessible to a worker in a wheelchair.

Reasonable accommodations do not include modifications that are primarily for the personal benefit of a worker with a disability. An employer generally need not provide a person whose leg has been amputated with a prosthetic limb or a paraplegic with a wheelchair. But if a personal item would specifically assist a person in performing the job, the employer should provide it, for example, specially designed eyeglasses that allow a visually impaired person to read a computer monitor.

There is no formula for making reasonable accommodation. Each worker, each disability, each employer, and each situation is unique; what is reasonable in one case may not be in another. Nevertheless, the following steps can lead an employer and a worker with a disability to a reasonable accommodation.

1. The employer must recognize the worker's disability. It is generally the worker's responsibility to inform the employer that an accommodation is needed. Of course, sometimes the disability is obvious, as when the worker is blind or uses a wheelchair. If a disability is not obvious, usually the worker will inform the employer of it because the worker cannot perform the job without accommodation. A worker who must have regular kidney dialysis might inform the employer of the need for

time off to have the therapy. On some occasions, a worker may be reluctant to identify a disability, but its presence becomes apparent to an employer. For example, an employer may realize that a worker is becoming hard of hearing and needs an amplifier for the telephone.

2. The employer must identify the barriers that interfere with the worker's performance. Of course, one of the best sources of information about these barriers is the worker. Barriers can be objects in the work environment, such as a door too narrow for a wheelchair to go through. Barriers can be specific functions of a job, such as speaking over the telephone for a hearing-impaired person. Other things can be barriers as well. For the worker who needs dialysis, a rigid work schedule would be a barrier.

3. All possible accommodations should be listed. The worker may suggest some. The employer may think of others. Agencies of government (for example, a state office of vocational rehabilitation or the EEOC) may have some ideas. Other employers may also be helpful.

4. The reasonableness of each possible accommodation must be assessed. *An accommodation is reasonable if it effectively provides the worker with a meaningful opportunity to achieve the same level of performance as a nondisabled person with similar skill and ability.* Such an accommodation must be reliable and available when needed. For example, one accommodation to the worker who needs dialysis would be to allow time off without pay, but this measure seems to prevent the worker from achieving the same level of performance as an able-bodied person. Perhaps a better accommodation (if possible in the job) would be to allow the worker to make up the time missed by coming to work early or leaving late.

5. Finally, a reasonable accommodation must be selected and put in place. The accommodation the worker wants should be used unless another accommodation is more effective or is equally effective but less expensive. No matter how effective, an accommodation is not required if it would impose an undue hardship on the business. (Undue hardship is discussed below.)

An accommodation need not be the best one possible (for example, the latest form of technology); an accommodation is reasonable if it effectively meets the job-related needs of the individual.

A worker with a disability need not accept an accommodation. If a worker rejects a reasonable accommodation and can perform the essential functions of the job, there should be no problem. For example, a person with a restricted field of vision may still be able to read and, therefore, reject an employer's offer of a reader. But if a worker rejects a reasonable accommodation and cannot perform the essential functions of the job, the worker is not qualified.

Here are additional examples of reasonable accommodations (which are often surprisingly inexpensive). Jobs can be restructured so that a nonessential function that a disabled worker cannot perform is assigned to another worker. (Fundamental change in the nature of the job is not required, however, and essential functions need not be reassigned.) A full-time job can be divided into part-time jobs to accommodate a qualified person (or persons) who cannot work all day or every day. Starting and quitting times can be adjusted to meet various needs; for instance, a worker who cannot drive may need to arrive late or leave early because of public transportation schedules. Special equipment may be helpful, such as magnifiers, talking calculators, and mechanical page turners. If a worker becomes unable to perform some essential functions of a job, and if reasonable accommodation is not feasible, the worker can be reassigned to another job in which the worker can perform the essential functions. Reassignment is available only to current employees, not to applicants.

Undue Hardship An employer need not make reasonable accommodation if it would impose an undue hardship on the business. Like reasonable accommodation, undue hardship is judged on the facts of each case. An undue hardship for one employer might not be for another; indeed, an undue hardship for an employer in one situation might not be an undue hardship for the same employer in another situation.

Obviously, high cost can be a hardship, but before making this determination, all available resources must be taken into account. Suppose a worker can perform the essential functions of a job only with the help of a device that costs $10,000. If the employer is the central office of a large and profitable corporation, the cost would probably not be a hardship. If the employer is a small and struggling new business, $10,000 would probably be too much to expect the employer to spend. In this case, the employer must look for other sources of funds. A state vocational rehabilitation agency might help pay for the device, and tax credits might help as well; also, the effect of normal income tax deductions must be figured in. Let us say that these sources together reduce the net cost of the device to $5,000. If this amount is still an undue burden, the worker must be given the option of paying part of the cost. If $4,000 is the maximum this employer could afford, the worker might contribute

$1,000 to bring the net cost to the employer down to a reasonable level.

Undue hardship may not be established merely by comparing the cost of accommodation to the disabled worker's salary. Nothing in the preceding example changes if the worker's annual pay is $15,000 or $100,000.

Cost is not the only form of hardship. The effect of accommodation on other workers may be taken into account. Suppose a die maker develops a disability that prevents her from performing some of the essential functions of her job, but she remains able to perform the job of machinist. If there are no openings for a machinist, the woman is not entitled to displace one. Now suppose there is an opening, but the seniority provisions of the collective bargaining agreement with the union give another worker the right to claim the job. Which worker has priority? A clear-cut answer does not exist. Reports in both the House of Representatives and the Senate indicated that seniority is relevant, but not controlling, on the question of hardship.

A fundamental change in the business can be an undue hardship. Suppose a waiter in a nightclub develops a vision impairment that makes it impossible for him to see in dim light. He asks his employer to install bright lighting. The cost might be small, but the change would destroy the ambience of the nightclub. Because the change would be fundamental, it is an undue hardship.

Simply that one accommodation is an undue hardship does not excuse the employer from making another accommodation that is not a hardship. Suppose the nightclub in the preceding example serves an outdoor lunch. The employer need not install bright lighting, but could transfer the waiter to the day shift.

Undue hardship cannot be justified on the basis of other employees' fears or prejudices concerning an individual's disability. Nor can undue hardship be justified merely because other employees are upset about the accommodation. Undue hardship could be demonstrated, however, if an accommodation interfered with the ability of other employees to perform their jobs.

Protection for Able-bodied Persons

The Disability Act protects able-bodied workers from discrimination based on their association with a disabled person. For example, an employer may not refuse to hire an applicant because the applicant's spouse has AIDS. An able-bodied worker is not entitled to reasonable accommodation, however, because another person is disabled. Thus, an able-bodied employee has no right to a modified work schedule to care for a spouse with a disability.

Like Title VII, the Disability Act also protects able-bodied workers from retaliation because they oppose practices that are illegal under the act or they file charges or otherwise participate in an investigation under the act.

Four Definitions of Discrimination

The definitions of discrimination under the Disability Act are similar to the definitions under Title VII. Here, we will look briefly at how the definitions operate under the Disability Act. Later, without regard to which definition may be involved, we will examine how the Disability Act is applied to several important issues.

Disparate Treatment

The essence of the first definition of discrimination, disparate treatment, is intent. An employer may not intentionally deny an employment opportunity to a qualified person with a disability. For example, an employer may not refuse to hire a qualified worker with a disability to avoid making reasonable accommodation. An employer may not refuse to hire a qualified applicant because the applicant has a record of having a disability (for example, a heart attack in the past). An employer may not refuse to hire a qualified applicant because the applicant is regarded as having a disability (for example, an erroneous belief that the applicant has tuberculosis). And an employer may not refuse to hire a qualified able-bodied applicant because the person is associated with a person with a disability; thus, an employer may not disqualify the parent of a chronically ill child or the spouse of a person with a disability in the belief that the applicant would miss too much work.

An employer may not reduce a worker's salary because the worker is disabled. An employer may not limit the duties or the opportunities for advancement of a worker with a disability. Perhaps the employer adopts the limitation in good faith, believing it to be in the best interest of the individual; nonetheless, the limitation is illegal. For example, an employer may not create separate promotion tracks for workers with disabilities or separate facilities such as offices or lunchrooms.

An employer must offer the same benefits to disabled workers as to able-bodied workers. Thus, an employer that offers counseling services for able-bodied workers must provide services for a deaf employee, for example, by hiring an interpreter.

An employer may not discharge a worker to avoid making reasonable accommodation. Thus, suppose a secretary's work has been fully satisfactory in the past. She suffers an accident and is restricted to a wheelchair, but she is able to do her work as well as before. The employer may not fire her to avoid making the workplace accessible.

The basic defense to a charge of disparate treatment is that the employer denied the worker an opportunity, not because of race, sex, or disability, but because of a legitimate reason. If two persons apply for a job, a qualified disabled person and a better qualified able-bodied person, and the employer hires the able-bodied one, disparate treatment has not occurred because the employer's reason—the desire to employ the better qualified person—is legitimate.

Disparate Impact

The second definition of discrimination is disparate impact. An employer may not maintain an employment practice or use a selection criterion that, although not intended to discriminate, has an adverse effect on workers with disabilities and is not justified by the needs of the business. Thus, all criteria used in hiring, promotion, and discharge—for example, written examinations, vision or hearing requirements, and strength tests—are subject to disparate impact analysis. If a criterion or practice screens out qualified workers with disabilities, it is illegal.

In a case under the Rehabilitation Act that Congress noticed, a worker applied to an apprenticeship program for the job of heavy-equipment operator. He had normal intelligence and coordination, but he had dyslexia and could not read well enough to pass a written examination for the program or to understand the training manual. Obviously, the test had a disparate impact on people with reading disabilities, and, because the employer did not attempt reasonable accommodation, the worker won the case.

The defense to a charge of disparate impact is that the practice is job-related and consistent with business necessity. Although the formal test validation procedures under Title VII are not necessary under the Disability Act, a practice or criterion must relate to an essential function of a job to justify a disparate impact. Suppose, for example, a blind and a sighted person apply for a job. The blind applicant is better qualified, yet the employer hires the sighted applicant because he has a driver's license and would be able to transport the employer if the employer's car broke down. The employer owns a new car, however, and trades it in every three years; therefore, being available to transport her is not an essential function of the job and not a defense to a charge of disparate impact.

In judging whether a practice is consistent with business necessity, reasonable accommodation must be taken into account. Suppose an employer interviews job applicants, and the interview is job-related. A deaf applicant is not allowed to interview because the employer does not know how to communicate with the applicant. Even though the interview is job-related, it will not serve as a defense in this case because a reasonable accommodation is readily available—providing an interpreter at the interview.

Reasonable Accommodation

The third definition of discrimination, reasonable accommodation, has already been discussed. It suffices here to note that the duty to make reasonable accommodation is much stronger under the Disability Act than under Title VII and that undue hardship is a reason for failing to make reasonable accommodation.

Retaliation

The fourth definition of discrimination is retaliation. An employer may not retaliate against a person (whether disabled or not) because the person has opposed an act or practice that is illegal under the Disability Act or because the person has filed a charge, given evidence, or otherwise participated in an investigation or hearing to enforce the act. An employer may not coerce, intimidate, threaten, harass, or interfere with anyone (disabled or not) who is exercising or enjoying any rights under the act or who is helping or encouraging someone else to exercise or enjoy these rights.

It is likely that the courts will follow the precedents under Title VII when deciding retaliation cases under the Disability Act. Therefore, see the discussion and illustrations of the law against retaliation in chapter 1.

Applications of the Disability Act

Preemployment Inquiries

An employer may not ask applicants, "Do you have any impairments or disabilities?" An employer may not give applicants a list of impairments and ask them to check off which they have. An employer may not ask about how an applicant became disabled or about the prognosis for a disability. An employer may, however, describe a job and ask whether an applicant can perform it *with or without* reasonable accommodation. An employer may state the attendance requirements of a job and ask whether an applicant can meet them, but the employer may not ask how often an applicant will have to miss work for treatment of an impairment. An employer may ask an applicant with a disability how the applicant, *with or without* reasonable accommodation, would be able to perform the essential functions of the job; for example, an employer may ask a person with one leg applying to repair home washing machines how the person would get up and down basement steps while carrying tools. An announcement that a test will be given may state that anyone who needs accommodation to take the test should inform the employer of this need and document it within a reasonable time.

An employer may ask a disabled applicant to demonstrate the ability to perform a function of a job. If the applicant cannot perform it without reasonable accommodation, the employer must attempt reasonable accommodation. The nature of the accommodation depends on whether the function is essential or marginal. If the function is essential, the employer must either provide the reasonable accommodation that the applicant needs or permit the applicant to explain how reasonable accommodation would facilitate effective job performance. If the function is marginal, the employer must provide a way for the worker to perform the function or transfer it to another job.

Medical Examinations

An employer generally may not require an applicant to take a medical examination *before* an offer of employment has been made. *After* an offer has been made, an employer may require workers to take a medical examination. The results of the examination must be kept confidential; they may be revealed only to persons who genuinely need to know them, for example, supervisors who must make reasonable accommodation and first-aid personnel.

A medical examination need not be job-related; however, if the employer withdraws an offer of employment to a disabled worker because the examination reveals the worker does not satisfy a criterion for the job, the employer must show that the criterion is job-related and consistent with business necessity and that no reasonable accommodation is possible. For example, suppose a worker applies for a job selling shoes. The employer offers the worker the job and sends her for a medical examination. It reveals that she has diabetes. This disease will not affect her ability to perform the job; therefore, the employer must hire the worker and not reveal unnecessarily that she is a diabetic.

Suppose, instead, the examination reveals that the worker has emphysema, which limits her ability to do vigorous exercise. In the employer's shoe store, much of the stock is kept in a basement, and clerks are required to go up and down the stairs many times each day. Furthermore, because customers are waiting, the clerks are expected to go up and down quickly. Thus, a job-related criterion for the position of clerk in this store is the ability to go up and down stairs often and quickly, and the medical examination reveals that the woman cannot meet this criterion. The employer must now attempt reasonable accommodation and, in the process, may consult with the store manager about the woman's impairment. Perhaps the function of climbing the stairs could be assigned to other workers. Perhaps a mechanical lift could be installed. Only if these (and any other) reasonable accommodations would impose an undue hardship may the employer withdraw the job offer.

Current workers may be required to take medical examinations to determine whether they are still able to perform the essential functions of their jobs, but current workers may not be required to take medical tests that are not job-related. Thus, a police department may require an officer to take a fitness-for-duty examination because an officer with, for example, a heart condition may be unable to pursue and apprehend suspects; but an employer who notices that a mechanic has suddenly lost a great deal of hair may not require the mechanic to be tested for cancer because being free of cancer is not essential to the job of mechanic.

Current workers may be given the opportunity to have voluntary medical examinations or to participate in wellness programs; these often take the form of screening for high blood pressure or cancer. The records of such examinations must be kept confidential.

Physical agility tests are not considered to be medical examinations and, therefore, may be given at any time. They must be given to all applicants or employees in a job class, not just to disabled workers. If such a test eliminates a person with a disability, the test must be job-related and consistent with business necessity.

Insurance

Congress seems to have intended that the theory of *disparate impact* would not apply to medical insurance or paid sick leave. These programs certainly can have a disparate impact on the disabled. For example, a clause in a medical insurance policy that excludes from coverage any conditions the worker had when hired (often called "preexisting conditions") will have a disparate impact on workers with disabilities because more disabled than able-bodied people have preexisting conditions.

Similarly, insurance policies often limit coverage for certain procedures such as blood transfusions, which may be limited to five each year. This limitation would have a disparate impact on a person with hemophilia, who may need more than five transfusions.

Along the same lines, a sick-leave policy might allow workers a maximum of ten paid sick days each year. This policy could have a disparate impact on a worker who needs kidney dialysis or therapy for a bad back.

Congress was aware of these examples and decided such restrictions are not illegal. Congress even decided that an employer may cut benefits—for example, reduce the amount of medical insurance or the number of paid sick days—as long as the employer's reason is not a desire to discriminate against the disabled. (A desire to save money on insurance costs is legal.)

Nevertheless, Congress did not intend to allow *disparate treatment* in insurance, leave, or any other benefit program. The same benefits must be available to disabled and able-bodied workers, unless the difference in benefits is based on sound actuarial principles. Thus, an employer may not exclude a person with a disability from an insurance program, nor may an employer include the person but impose a lower cap on benefits. Accordingly, an insurance plan may reimburse a person with hemophilia for a maximum of five transfusions a year, but the same maximum must apply to able-bodied workers. Similarly, the plan may not deny a hemophiliac coverage for heart surgery if this procedure is available to other workers. An employer that allows able-bodied workers to take a certain number of paid leave days may not specify fewer days for persons with disabilities.

An employer may not refuse to hire a person with a disability on the ground that the employer's premiums for workers' compensation or medical or other insurance would increase.

Able-bodied persons are protected against discrimination based on their association with disabled persons. As a result, an employer that provides medical insurance benefits for the dependents of workers may not exclude, or reduce coverage for, dependents who are disabled (and this rule holds even if full coverage would increase medical insurance costs).

Drug Testing

The Disability Act is neutral toward drug testing; the act does not encourage, authorize, or prohibit drug testing. Drug tests are not considered medical examinations under the act.

Remedies and Procedures for Enforcement

The Disability Act incorporates the remedies and procedures of Title VII. Thus, a person who believes oneself to be a victim of discrimination must file a charge with a local agency if one exists, must file a charge with the EEOC, and may eventually file a suit in court. The statutes of limitations under the Disability Act are the same as under Title VII. If a lawsuit is successful, the victim may receive back pay, compensation for economic and emotional losses, attorney's fees, and punitive damages for malicious violations. The victim may also benefit from an injunction.

4
The Equal Pay Act

The first federal law to guarantee equality of opportunity was the Equal Pay Act of 1963. It requires that an employer pay a man and a woman at the same rate when they are performing equal work. This is a narrow protection. Under this law, an employer remains free to refuse to hire women, free to hire and segregate them into "women's jobs," and free to harass or discharge them simply because they are women. (Of course, all of these acts are outlawed by Title VII.)

The requirement of equal pay for equal work comports with economics as well as justice. If two persons do equal work (all other things being equal), each deserves the same compensation, and the employer would be wasting money to pay one more than the other.

The actual requirements of the Equal Pay Act are somewhat more complex than just indicated. Stated more fully, the act prohibits a covered employer from paying a person of one sex at a lower rate than a person of the other sex for the performance of equal work on jobs that require equal skill, effort, and responsibility and that are performed under similar working conditions in the same establishment, unless the differential in pay is based on seniority, merit, the quantity or quality of production, or any other factor except sex. This chapter discusses these requirements in detail.

Who Must Obey the Equal Pay Act

The Equal Pay Act is part of the Fair Labor Standards Act, and, with one exception, the coverage of these two laws is the same. Therefore, if an employer is required to pay a worker the federal minimum wage and time-and-a-half for work in excess of forty hours in a week, the employer is also obliged to obey the Equal Pay Act regarding that worker. The one exception is favorable to workers. The Fair Labor Standards Act does not protect executives, administrators, or professionals, but the Equal Pay Act does.

Some employers are excluded from coverage. Whether a particular employer is excluded depends on a number of specific rules and the facts of each case. Without going into the details, we can offer a few illustrative statements about coverage.

On the whole, large private employers are covered by the Equal Pay Act, but small employers are not. For example, retail and service businesses with annual sales of less than $360,000 (such as most barbershops and boutiques) are not covered. Small farms are not covered. Recreational facilities, such as amusement parks, golf courses, theaters, and ball parks, are not covered if they are open less than seven months a year. Small regional newspapers are not covered.

State and local governments are covered by the act. So are schools and hospitals, whether public or private.

Comparisons between employers are not permitted. If Mr. A owns a private men's club and pays his all-male staff $7 an hour, and Ms. B owns a private women's club across the street and pays her all-female staff only $6 an hour for the same work, the law is not violated.

Similarly, comparisons between different establishments owned by the same employer are not permitted. Suppose an employer owns a grocery store and a sporting goods shop. Each establishment employs a full-time cash register operator. If the employer pays the male operator in the sporting goods shop more than the female operator in the grocery store, the Equal Pay Act is not offended, even if their work is equal.

Physical separation is an important fact in deciding whether two places of business owned by the same employer are different establishments. For example, suppose an employer owns two department stores, each covered by the act. The stores are on opposite sides of town, and each store has its own management. If a female clerk in one store is paid less than a male clerk doing the same work in the other store, the law is not violated because the workers are in different establishments.

Physical separation is not the only important fact, however, in deciding whether establishments are separate. Centralization of administration can also count heavily. The schools in a district may be physically separate from one another, but they usually constitute a single establishment because personnel policies are made and administered from a central office.

A final word about coverage: state equal pay laws cover many employers that the federal law does not. For example, the New York Human

Rights Act, which requires equal pay, applies to employers of four or more employees.

Who Is Protected by the Equal Pay Act

In general, a worker who is employed by an employer that must obey the Equal Pay Act is protected, but a few exceptions apply. Elected officials of state and local governments, members of their personal staffs, the persons they appoint to policy-making positions, and their legal advisers are not protected by the act. Although most federal employees are protected, uniformed military personnel and employees of Congress are not.

As we turn to a discussion of what the Equal Pay Act permits and prohibits, we should note that, in the examples in this chapter, the underpaid person is always a woman. The reason is that, in our society, the underpaid person is (almost) always a woman. Nevertheless, the law protects both sexes. If an employer pays a man less than a woman for equal work, the law is violated.

The Comparator

To establish a violation of the Equal Pay Act, a woman must compare her job to a man's job. The man is called her "comparator." Two issues have arisen concerning the woman and her comparator. The first is, Must they be employed in the establishment at the same time? The answer is no, as long as their jobs are equal. For example, suppose an employer pays a man $10 an hour for a job. When the man resigns, the employer hires a woman for the job—and pays her only $8 an hour. The employer has violated the law (unless a factor other than sex explains the differential).

The second issue concerning comparators arises when several men hold the same job title, but receive different rates of pay (and the differences are not justified by seniority, merit, or another legitimate reason). Some or all of the men earn more than a woman who claims that her job is equal to theirs. For example, suppose a male "machinist" is paid $15 an hour. Three other male machinists are paid $13 an hour, and one is paid $11 an hour. All the men perform the same work. A female "machine operator," whose work is equal to the men's, is paid $13 an hour. The courts agree that the woman does not lose her case merely because a man is paid less than she for equal work. (Indeed, the man earning only $11 an hour has a valid claim against the employer because the woman is paid more than he for equal work!)

The courts divide on how to deal with the range of the men's pay.

The woman, of course, prefers to choose the man earning $15 an hour as her comparator, and some courts permit her to do so. Other courts, however, require her to compare her pay to the average of the men's pay. In these courts, the woman in our example would lose her case because her pay is equal to the average of the men's pay.

Equal Pay

Pay includes all kinds of compensation. It includes not only the stated wage or salary, but also fringe benefits such as medical care and vacations, as well as deferred compensation such as pensions.

The Equal Pay Act requires that a man and a woman who perform equal work receive the same *rate of pay*, for example, $15 dollars an hour, $30,000 a year, $5 per garment, or 12 percent of gross sales. Take-home pay, therefore, may vary. Suppose a male machinist is paid $15 an hour and works forty hours in a week. His gross weekly pay is $600. A female machinist is also paid $15 an hour, but she works only thirty-five hours in a week. Her gross pay is $525. Although the man's take-home pay exceeds the woman's, the employer has complied with the Equal Pay Act because their rates of pay are the same.

Similarly, hours worked may vary. Suppose a male and a female architect are each paid $45,000 a year. The man is a faster worker, and, as a result, the woman spends more hours on the job. The employer has satisfied the act because the workers' rates of pay are the same.

An employer can violate the act if the woman's rate of pay is lower than the man's, even if their take-home pay is the same. An employer operated a health spa that separated male and female customers. The male managers of the men's division were paid 7.5 percent of gross sales, whereas the female managers of the women's division were paid only 5 percent of gross. Yet, because there were more female customers, the paychecks of the male and female managers turned out to be equal. The court held that the employer violated the act because the male and female managers' rates of pay should have been equal. (If the rates had been equal, the women would have earned more than the men. The act would not have been offended because the women's higher pay would have been based on the profits their work generated.)

Equal Work

The Equal Pay Act applies only if the woman and her comparator are performing equal work. It is necessary, therefore, to compare the woman's work with the man's work. In the typical case, the jobs they hold have different titles. Accordingly, we will speak of them as different jobs, though we recognize that the woman is trying to prove that they are basically the same. The act specifies the criteria for making the comparison, that is, for deciding whether work is equal; the criteria are skill, effort, responsibility, and working conditions.

Before we discuss these criteria, it is well to note that the act focuses on the work performed, not on the individuals performing it. Suppose Mario holds a college degree, whereas Maria did not finish high school. If they are both pumping gas in a service station, they are entitled to the same pay; Mario's additional credentials are irrelevant to the job. Similarly, suppose Claudio and Claudia are fraternal twins who are indistinguishable except for sex. They work for the same employer but in different jobs. The act does not require that they be paid equally, even though their talents, education, interests, and so forth are identical.

Also, the act is concerned with work that is actually performed, not with work that exists in a plan or job description. Of course, the duties listed in a job description are evidence of the work that is performed, but the controlling facts are what the workers actually do on the job. In the usual case, the jobs that the woman and her comparator hold are classified by the employer as being different, and the job descriptions identify at least a few different duties. But if the woman proves that the jobs in fact call for equal skill, effort, and responsibility and are performed under similar working conditions (and the employer fails to prove that seniority, merit, or some other legitimate factor justifies the pay differential), the jobs are deemed equal and the woman is entitled to the same pay as the man.

Now let us turn to the criteria that define equal work.

Skill

Skill is the ability needed to perform the duties of a job. The elements of skill include the levels of education, training, experience, and natural ability that are necessary to the job. The skill of a tailor who alters men's clothes in a clothing store is equal to the skill of a seamstress who alters women's clothes in the same store.

Skill does not include the efficiency of the individuals who perform the duties. The tailor might work twice as fast as the seamstress (and, for this reason, might rightfully earn more pay), but he would not be more skilled than she.

Effort

Effort is the physical and mental exertion needed to perform the duties of a job. Writing original stories requires more effort than writing summaries of published stories. Lifting one hundred pounds requires more effort than lifting twenty-five pounds.

Women have argued that a woman's job may require frequent movement of small weights (mopping floors, emptying wastebaskets), and a man's job may require occasional movement of large weights (lifting full garbage cans, operating a heavy machine), but the effort for the two jobs is equal because the woman moves as much total weight in a day as her comparator. The courts have not accepted this argument, however. They have held that the man's job requires more effort.

The courts have also rejected the argument that the effort required in jobs is equal if a woman is just as tired at the end of the day as her comparator. This argument mistakenly looks at the worker, not the job. Washing windows might tire a 125-pound woman as much as playing football tires a 250-pound man. As measured by her abilities, perhaps the woman is expending as much effort as her comparator. Nevertheless, the act focuses on jobs, not workers, and the man's job requires more effort than the woman's.

Equal effort may be needed in jobs even though some duties are different. Often, many of the duties of a woman's job and a man's job are the same, but each job has some duties not shared by the other. Suppose a female secretary and a male administrative aide both type letters and take and deliver messages; but only the aide makes travel arrangements and keeps track of and orders office supplies, and only the secretary goes to the post office and to the bank. The effort needed in jobs is equal, of course, to the extent that the jobs share duties. Whether the overall effort needed for the two jobs is equal depends on how much time is spent on the unshared duties and how similar these duties are. Making travel arrangements probably requires no more effort than going to the post office or bank, but keeping track of and ordering supplies might require more effort. Whether effort for the secretary is equal to effort for the aide depends, therefore, on how difficult it is to keep track of and order supplies in this firm.

Responsibility

Responsibility is the extent to which a worker supervises other workers, makes important decisions, or is accountable for the success of the business. The law uses the ordinary meaning of supervising other workers, but, to justify a pay differential, supervision must involve genuine power and occur on a regular basis. The employer in the preceding paragraph could not justify paying the administrative aide more because he is in charge "in case of an emergency" or occasionally delegates work to others.

Decision making means making important choices and being held accountable to higher authority for the success of those choices. A pay differential for the aide could not be justified on the ground that he has authority to decide from which supplier to buy products when their prices are equal, for the decision is minor.

Accountability for the success of the firm refers to how important the worker's performance is to the business. A deputy sheriff who enforces the law has more responsibility than a jailer who watches over prisoners. A clerk who controls a warehouse is more accountable than one who controls a supply room. If the administrative aide in our example had authority to authorize checks in payment for supplies, he would have more responsibility than the secretary.

Responsibility comes in varying degrees. An employer may seek to justify a pay differential on the ground that, although both the man and the woman have responsibilities, the man's are greater. If such a claim is made in regard to supervising other workers, the relevant facts would include the number of persons supervised and the degree of power exercised. Supervising one hundred workers involves more responsibility than supervising ten, and having power to discharge involves more responsibility than having power to put notes in a personnel file.

If an employer seeks to justify a differential based on decision making or accountability for the success of the firm, the relevant facts would include the importance of the decisions and how often they are made. The decisions that our administrative aide makes about which airlines and hotels to use for his boss's travels are probably no more important than the decisions the secretary makes about which overnight courier to use. If, however, the aide decides which computer system to purchase, his job carries more responsibility than hers.

Working Conditions

The fourth criterion, working conditions, differs from the preceding three criteria in two ways. The first way is that whereas "skill," "effort," and "responsibility" carry their ordinary English meanings in the act, "working conditions" is a term of art. Congress deliberately adopted the technical meaning of this term as it is used in the field of industrial relations.

The technical meaning of "working conditions" refers to surroundings and hazards. Surroundings include elements with which a worker comes in contact on the job, such as toxic chemicals or fumes. The more frequent and intense the contact, the worse the surroundings. Hazards include physical dangers that a worker encounters on the job, such as working at heights or with high voltage lines. Again, the more frequent and severe the dangers, the worse the hazards.

According to this meaning, the night shift is performed under the same working conditions as the day shift because the surroundings and hazards are the same. A job in a room with a window is performed under the same working conditions as a job in a room without a window, however much people might prefer the room with the window. But a male sales representative who travels to customers' stores works under different conditions from a female sales representative who waits in a factory for customers to come to her. Likewise, a job in a high-crime area has worse working conditions than a job in a quiet suburb.

The second way in which the criterion of working conditions differs from the other three criteria is that the working conditions need only be similar, not equal. Being exposed to one toxic chemical is not exactly equal to being exposed to another toxic chemical, but the working conditions may still be similar. Repairing roofs is not exactly equal to painting on a tall ladder, but the risks are similar and, in all probability, so are the working conditions.

Substantial Equality

If the Equal Pay Act were interpreted narrowly by the courts, an employer who wished to discriminate could pay a man's job more than a woman's job merely by assigning one or two minor extra duties to the man's job. Judges are sensitive to such strategies to evade the purpose of the law. Therefore, two jobs need not be identical to be covered by the act. Equal pay is required if the man's and the woman's jobs are *substantially equal.* Nonetheless, a man's job and a woman's job may have some duties in common yet be genuinely different jobs. As a result, Equal Pay Act cases often require the courts to decide whether two jobs that share some duties entail equal work.

In essence, the shared duties must be weighed against the unshared duties to see which set predominates. The criteria used in the weighing process are the ones we have discussed—skill, effort, responsibility, and working conditions. In addition, the courts consider the numbers of shared and unshared duties, the regularity of their performance, and the time the workers spend performing them.

Cases at the extremes are easily decided. If there are six shared and five unshared duties, the unshared duties require different levels of skill and effort, and the unshared duties consume three hours every day, the jobs are different. If there are four shared and two unshared duties, the unshared duties require similar levels of skill and effort, and the unshared duties are performed once a week for half an hour, the jobs are equal. But most cases fall between these extremes, and reasonable people can differ about whether the shared or the unshared duties predominate.

Comparable Worth

All four criteria of equal work must be satisfied to establish a violation of the Equal Pay Act. The criteria may not be balanced against one another. Thus, if the man's job requires more effort, but the woman's job carries more responsibility, the man and the woman are not performing equal work. The extra responsibility of the woman's job does not compensate for its lesser effort.

Balancing the criteria of equal work against one another would be a long step toward adopting comparable worth. Comparable worth is the doctrine that jobs should be paid according to their worth to the firm. If two jobs require different skills, degrees of effort, and so on, yet they are equally valuable to the firm, advocates of comparable worth argue that the jobs should receive the same pay. Value to the firm is determined by job evaluation plans, which typically assign points to jobs according to the levels of skill, effort, and so on that are required to perform the jobs. Thus, it is possible that strikingly different jobs—for example, mechanic and secretary—are equally valuable to the firm in the sense that they receive equal points. The mechanic may exert more effort, but the secretary has more responsibility, so that the point totals are the same.

Comparable worth is a controversial doctrine. Its advocates are often feminists because when two jobs score equal points, the job held by women is commonly paid less than the job held by men. Yet the legislative history of the Equal Pay Act indicates that Congress did not intend to adopt this doctrine, and the federal courts have rejected it.

Defenses

An employer may pay a man at a higher rate than a woman for equal work if the difference in pay is based on a legitimate factor. The act names three legitimate factors—seniority, merit, and piece rates—and recognizes that others might exist.

Seniority

If an employer follows a seniority system that awards higher pay to workers with longer service, a senior man may be paid more than a junior woman for equal work. To use the defense of seniority, the employer must have a genuine system, and it must operate according to rules. If an employer sometimes rewards seniority and sometimes does not, the employer does not have a true seniority system, and it cannot be used to justify paying a woman less than a man for equal work. Thus, suppose the starting pay for assemblers is $8 an hour. This rate is raised $.05 per hour for each year of service with the company. Carlos has been an assembler for twenty years and makes $9 an hour. Carol has been an assembler for ten years and makes only $8.50 per hour. The difference in pay is legal because it is based on a seniority system that has rules that are regularly followed.

Further, the system itself must not discriminate against women. Thus, in the example in the preceding paragraph, if another woman, Karen, had twenty years of service but was paid less than Carlos, the differentials—both Karen's and Carol's—would be illegal because the system was discriminatory.

Merit Pay and Piece Rates

A man may be paid more than a woman if he is more productive than she. Piece rates exemplify pay according to productivity. If male and female workers are paid $5 for each shirt they produce, their rates of pay are equal and the Equal Pay Act is satisfied. If Elijah sews ten shirts in one day and Eliza sews nine, he is more productive that day and is rightfully paid more money.

A worker's merit or productivity is often determined according to a supervisor's opinion, for example, "Harold is more productive than Henrietta" or "Harold is a better worker than Henrietta." Subjective judgments like these are not illegal, but they are a weak basis for a pay differential because they are easily infected by prejudicial attitudes. If an employer wishes to reward more productive workers, it is wise to identify the important features of the job and devise objective scales for evaluating performance.

Factors Other Than Sex

The Equal Pay Act is aimed at eradicating one form of sex discrimination. It follows that the act does not prohibit a pay differential that is based on factors other than sex. An employer may pay his brother more than a woman in the same job because the basis of the differential is family status, not sex.

Following are additional examples of factors other than sex.

Shift Differentials An employer may pay a man on the night shift more than a woman in the same job on the day shift. (As we noted above, the working conditions for day and night jobs are the same. Time of day, however, is a factor other than sex and may be the basis for a pay differential.)

Part-Time Employment A part-time female worker may be paid less than a full-time male in the same job.

Training Programs A man who performs a job as a step in a training program may be paid more than a woman who regularly performs the same job. For example, a man in training to become an officer of a bank may be assigned to work as a teller for a few weeks. As an officer-in-training, he may legally be paid more than a female teller, though for this period their work is equal. A danger of training programs is that an employer who wishes to evade the act can easily say that a man is paid more than a woman because he is "in training for future promotion." To avoid this danger, the courts have held that a training program can justify a pay differential only if four requirements are satisfied: (1) the program includes formal instruction of trainees; (2) trainees are rotated regularly through jobs; (3) the program has a clearly defined ending point; and (4) successful trainees are placed in a specific job. Also, the program must not be discriminatory; if women are excluded from the program, it cannot justify a differential in pay.

Education or Experience A man may be paid more than a woman if he has more or better relevant education or experience. This factor is often coupled with starting pay. For example, suppose an engineering firm recruits two persons in the same year: a man graduating from the nation's top school and a woman graduating from a less prestigious school. To attract the man, whom several other firms are also recruiting, the employer offers him a higher starting salary than it offers the woman, who was not heavily recruited. In the next five years, they receive equal raises. The result is that, although their work is equal, he receives more pay than the woman at all times. The difference in pay the first year is justified by the man's superior education, and the differential thereafter is justified by the difference in starting pay.

Two factors that might seem to be factors other than sex, and thus to justify a pay differential, have been rejected by the courts. The first factor is the average cost of employing men and women. For a given employer, it could be more costly to employ women because of medical insurance rates or the need to install new restrooms. Nevertheless, the law requires that workers be judged as individuals, not as members of groups. An employer owes equal pay to men and women doing equal work, regardless of average costs.

The second factor is the labor market. An employer may not pay a woman less than a man merely because she is willing to accept the job at lower pay. It might be argued that the employer did not force the woman to take the job; that if she is willing to do the work for less than a man, the law should not be concerned. This argument, which is known as the "market defense," has been answered with a powerful counterargument: society has discriminated against women for generations. If men demand a certain rate of pay for a certain job, why would women perform the same work for less money? The reason is discrimination, and it is not a legitimate reason. The market defense has failed in court. If it had been accepted, the Equal Pay Act would have become almost meaningless.

Procedures for Bringing a Claim and Remedies

The Equal Pay Act is enforced by lawsuits. The suit must be filed within two years of the discriminatory act. (This period is extended to three years if the employer willfully violated the act. Willfulness, which is difficult to prove, means the employer knew the act applied and deliberately disregarded it.) No charge needs to be filed with the government.

The basic remedy for a violation of the act is back pay, which is the difference between what the plaintiff and her comparator earned. In addition, the plaintiff may be entitled to liquidated damages, which is a sum of money ranging from as little as $1 to as much as the amount of back pay owed. The judge has discretion to reduce or eliminate liquidated damages (but not back pay) if the employer acted reasonably and in good faith. Other damages (such as compensation for emotional suffering and punitive damages) are not available, but attorney's fees are. In addition, the employer must raise the woman's pay to equal her comparator's; the employer may not lower the comparator's pay.

5
Other Statutes

In addition to the statutes already discussed, several other laws protect workers against discrimination. This chapter briefly describes some of those laws.

Local Laws

Although this bulletin focuses on federal law, it is important to be aware of the law of cities and states ("local laws"). In general, the federal laws against employment discrimination do not supersede or override local laws against discrimination; we are obliged to obey all of them. If, however, a local law authorizes behavior that a federal law prohibits (for example, prohibiting women from working more than eight hours a day), the local law is invalid.

Local laws can give greater protection than federal law in three ways. The New York Human Rights Law illustrates all three of these ways.

The first way is that a local law can prohibit conduct that the federal law does not prohibit. For example, Title VII prohibits discrimination based on race, but does not prohibit discrimination based on marital status. Suppose a covered employer in New York refuses to hire an African-American man because of his race; the employer also refuses to hire a woman because she is married. The refusal to hire the man because of his race violates Title VII. The refusal to hire the woman because she is married does *not* violate Title VII. The New York Human Rights Act, however, prohibits discrimination based on marital status; therefore, the refusal to hire the married woman violates *state* law. Alabama lacks a law against employment discrimination by private employers. If the employer is in Alabama, the refusal to hire the African-American man is still illegal because federal law applies in all states; but the refusal to hire the married woman is not unlawful there.

The second way that local laws can give greater protection than federal law is by covering more employers. For example, after July 1994, the Disability Act will apply to firms that have at least fifteen employees. Consequently, an employer with ten employees would not violate the Disability Act by refusing to make reasonable accommodation to a qualified person with a disability. But if that employer were in New York, the refusal would be illegal because the New York law applies to firms with four or more employees.

The third way that local laws can give greater protection than federal law is by covering more workers. For example, suppose an employer in New York says to a twenty-year-old applicant, "You are too young for this job." The Age Act only protects workers who are at least forty years old, so this employer has not violated federal law. But the New York Human Rights Act protects workers between the ages of eighteen and sixty-five from age discrimination, so this employer has violated local law.

National Labor Relations Act

The National Labor Relations Act (also known as the Labor Management Relations Act or the Taft-Hartley Act) protects workers against discrimination based on concerted activity. "Concerted activity" is the right of workers to act together to improve their working lives. It includes the rights

- to form, join, or assist labor unions (as well as the right to refrain from these activities)

- to discuss or bargain collectively with an employer over terms and conditions of employment;

- to enforce a collective bargaining agreement, for example, to file a grievance or go to arbitration; and

- to picket and to strike.

It is an unfair labor practice for an employer to discriminate against workers who engage in concerted activity. For example, an employer may not discipline or discharge workers because they have encouraged other workers to join a union.

The Labor Act also protects workers against discrimination by unions. A union may not discriminate against workers because they have engaged in, or refused to engage in, concerted activity. For example, if a worker holds a job in a bargaining unit represented by a union, the union may not decline to process the worker's grievances merely because the worker has not joined the union. It is also an unfair labor practice for a union to discriminate against a worker because of the worker's race or sex.

The Labor Act is enforced by the National Labor Relations Board. Workers who believe they have been discriminated against because of concerted activity must file a charge with a regional office of the Labor Board.

The Constitution

Federal, state, and local governments are prohibited by their constitutions from discriminating against workers on many bases. In general, an agency of government may not discriminate against its employees on any basis that is not related to job performance. Federal constitutional law is too complex, and state constitutions too varied, for detailed discussion in this bulletin; but a few words about the federal Constitution are possible.

The federal Constitution prohibits disparate treatment, but not disparate impact discrimination. The Constitution prohibits unjustified disparate treatment of employees of government on many bases; some of these bases go beyond the statutes discussed in earlier chapters of this bulletin. Thus, the Constitution protects government employees against discrimination not only on the bases of race, sex, and so on, but also on the bases of speech, association, marital status, and sexual preference.

The word "unjustified" in the preceding paragraph is important. The government may discriminate against its employees if the discrimination is justifiable. For example, the government may require combat pilots to retire from their jobs at a certain age.

The Constitution provides employees of government an additional protection: due process of law. The government may not discipline or discharge workers without notifying them of the charges and giving them an opportunity to defend themselves. In the private sector, only unionized workers enjoy these protections.

Section 1981

In the aftermath of the Civil War, Congress enacted a law providing that "all persons . . . shall have the same right . . . to make and enforce contracts . . . as is enjoyed by white citizens." This law is known today as 42 U.S.C. section 1981. It protects workers against employment discrimination because the employment relationship is a kind of contract.

Section 1981 and Title VII are both in effect today. They overlap to some extent, but they differ in significant ways.

Section 1981 is much narrower than Title VII in two respects. The words "the same right . . . as . . . white citizens" mean that section 1981 applies only to race discrimination and cannot be invoked against discrimination on the basis of religion, sex, age, and so on. Also, section 1981 bans only intentional discrimination, that is, disparate treatment; the statute does not ban disparate impact or the other kinds of discrimination outlawed by Title VII.

Section 1981 and Title VII overlap in that both cover all phases of the employment relationship. The original language of section 1981 referred to making and enforcing contracts. Recently, the Supreme Court read this language narrowly, holding it applied only to the act of hiring and not to anything afterward—therefore, not to racial harassment, failure to promote, or discharge. Congress swiftly amended the statute to broaden its coverage. Today both section 1981 and Title VII cover the employment relationship from hiring to pensions.

Section 1981 is broader than Title VII in one way. Whereas Title VII applies only to employers of fifteen or more employees, section 1981 applies to all employers, regardless of size. Therefore, section 1981 protects workers against racial discrimination by the smallest of businesses.

The procedures under section 1981 and Title VII also differ. Section 1981 can be enforced directly and immediately by the courts. Whereas Title VII requires that charges be filed with local agencies and with the EEOC, so that several months must pass before a lawsuit can be filed, section 1981 is enforced the old-fashioned way: one simply files a lawsuit—and one may do so the day after the racial discrimination occurs.

Finally, section 1981 neither contains its own limitations period nor is covered by any other federal statute of limitations. As a result, the courts apply a statute of limitations of the state in which the case is filed. The Supreme Court has held that the statute of limitations for personal injury actions is the appropriate one to use.

Immigration Act of 1986

The Immigration Reform and Control Act of 1986 applies to employers of four or more employees. This act makes it illegal for an employer to hire undocumented aliens. Because Title VII does not prohibit employment discrimination on the ground of citizenship, Congress feared that employers, in their zeal to obey the Immigration Act, would refuse to hire non-American citizens (and perhaps even Americans with unfamiliar names or foreign appearances). As a result, the Immigration Act makes it illegal for an employer to discriminate on the basis of citizenship against United States citizens and persons in the process of becoming citizens.

Afterword

The journey on which Rosa Parks launched us in 1957 is not complete. Other oppressed classes clamor for legal protection, and classes that are already protected say the laws are not enforced vigorously enough. Although we have come a long way, our future as a moral people and as a productive nation depends on our effort to achieve equality of opportunity for every worker. We can achieve this goal. Our destiny is in our own hands and hearts.

Other Recent ILR Bulletins

Auditing Local Union Financial Records: A Guide for Local Union Trustees
by John Lund (1992, 96 pages, $9.95)
> "Valuable both as a text in the classroom and as a reference that belongs on the shelf at every local union."—*Thomas E. Seay, Bond, Beebe, Barton and Muckelbauer, P.C.*

Industrial and Labor Relations Terms: A Glossary
by Robert E. Doherty (1989, 5th edition, 40 pages, $4.95)
> Revised to reflect recent developments in labor relations, the fifth edition of this popular reference book gives definitions and historical background for about 300 frequently used words, phrases, and acronyms. It is extensively cross-referenced.

An Introduction to Labor Law
by Michael Evan Gold (1989, 72 pages, $7.95)
> "Does an excellent job of explaining complex labor concepts in a way which is both accurate and understandable."—*Julius G. Getman, University of Texas School of Law*

To order or to request a free catalog of publications, please contact:
ILR Press
School of Industrial and Labor Relations
Cornell University
Ithaca, NY 14853-3901
Telephone: 607/255-2264